Anglesey
Villages

Margaret Hughes

ISBN: 0-86381-814-5
Cover design: Sian Parri

First published in 2003 by
Gwasg Carreg Gwalch, 12 Iard yr Orsaf, Llanrwst, Wales LL26 0EH
℡ 01492 642031 🖷 01492 641502
🖱 books@carreg-gwalch.co.uk   Internet: www.carreg-gwalch.co.uk

In memory of my parents
William and Mary Owen, Manchester

Acknowledgement

A book such as *Anglesey Villages* cannot be compiled without the assistance of many people, past and present. I am indebted to the staffs of Llangefni Library and the Archives office at Llangefni for help in tracing much of the information . . .

. . . and to the many authors, so much more knowledgeable than I, whose books I have read . . .

Councillor Gwyn Jones of Dwyran was a mine of information about the Prichard-Jones Institute; John Rowlands of Pont-Rhyd-Bont has been generous in his support, as ever . . .

. . . and once more, Gwasg Carreg Gwalch has reproduced my text with patience and skill in the friendliest fashion.

Contents

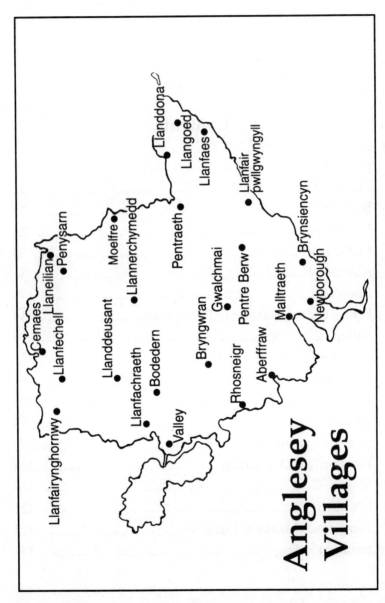

Anglesey
Villages

Llanddona
Llangoed
Llanfaes
Llanfair pwllgwyngyll
Brynsiencyn
Newborough
Malltraeth
Pentre Berw
Gwalchmai
Pentraeth
Bryngwran
Aberffraw
Rhosneigr
Moelfre
Llannerchymedd
Penysarn
Llaneilian
Llanfechell
Cemaes
Llanddeusant
Bodedern
Llanfachraeth
Valley
Llanfairynghornwy

Introduction

At first glance there seems little to commend Anglesey villages, considered in terms of the quality of architecture which makes Cotswold villages, say, so attractive. Many of them appear to be a huddle of nondescript cottages, small terraces and grey chapels which, over a period of years, have been refurbished then left to decline, and refurbished again, the latest innovation being plastic replacement windows and doors and rough-casting, all of which have the effect of de-characterisation and creating boring uniformity.

Hardly a subject for a book, you may think. Yet each village discussed in the following pages has features which set it apart from its neighbour up the road or across the fields. Features created by history, topography, and centuries of living, none of which is immediately apparent to the visitor.

How to define a village? Indeed, when does a hamlet become a village, a village a town? The boundaries are blurred if one is content to abide by the definition in the dictionary.

For the sake of this book, a village may have a shop, a church, a chapel or two, a school, a public house, and, maybe, a village hall. One, two, three or all of these amenities. It may have a parish council and possibly a community council. It does not boast the importance of a town hall or a town council.

The village will be under the watchful eye of an elected county councillor, and its expansion (or, in some cases, dereliction) is answerable to planning authority regulations from above.

Move home from one village in Anglesey to another, and one soon senses a subtle difference in character, a lack of uniformity.

To know Anglesey in depth, acquaintance of its towns and resorts and scenery is not enough. One must know its villages and the events and the people which have made them what they are today.

Llanfair Pwllgwyngyll

The village of Llanfair Pwllgwyngyll, a development along the old Holyhead road as it leaves the Menai Strait towards the port at Holyhead, with newer residential property to the north east, is marked at one end by the Anglesey Column and at the other end by the railway station and Pringle's department store. In between lies one of the largest areas of village housing in Anglesey, a dormitory for workers in Bangor (the University, colleges, schools, hospital and commercial enterprises) and Llangefni (local government offices, college, and industrial estate).

Before the days of Thomas Telford and his road-building, Llanfair Pwllgwyngyll would have been more correctly termed a hamlet. It was a cluster of cottages on the higher ground behind the rock on which the Anglesey Column now stands, an area known today as the upper village.

As much of the land hereabouts was owned by the Paget family of Plas Newydd, whose illustrious member, Henry William Paget, was wounded and lost a leg at the battle of Waterloo in 1815, and who was later created 1st Marquess of Anglesey, it was only to be expected that any memorial to him should be erected to stand prominent on his own land. The 28m column of Moelfre stone was built in 1817, and five years after his death, in 1860, London sculptor Matthew Noble completed the massive bronze figure, which must have aroused great interest as it was hoisted up to its plinth.

Today's visitors who climb the 115 steps inside the column to the balcony are rewarded with a stupendous view south and west across the village to the Llŷn peninsula, to Snowdon and the mountains of Eryri, east towards the Great Orme, and north across the rolling green countryside of Anglesey.

As is the case with many Anglesey villages, the parish church lies some distance away. The first church has disappeared long since, but the present building, dated 1851-2, stands on the same site on the edge of the Strait and is said to have some of the early stones in its walls. The early Christian saints who founded many of Anglesey's churches chose sites close to the shore. The church of St Mary lies immediately below the great stone structure of the Britannia Bridge, reached along the quiet country lane leading past the Carreg Brân Hotel, under the railway, down to the shore. Close by the churchyard wall is a memorial to those who lost their lives while working on the bridge during the middle of the 19th century, and more recently when the bridge was re-built during the 1970's, following the fire which destroyed the original tubular railway crossing.

A path through the churchyard leads to the shore ad the statue of Horatio Nelson, designed by Admiral Lord Clarence Paget, fourth son of the 1st Marquess, who was Admiral of the Fleet in the Mediterranean and naval secretary from 1859 to 1866. His interests lay in the arts, including sculpture, and he made what must have been one of the earliest uses of concrete using Portland cement to build the statue. It was unveiled in 1873 and intended as a landmark for sailors.

The tongue-twister name, LlanfairPwllgwyngyllgo gerychwyrn-drobwllllantisiliogogogoch, which intrigues visitors, is not the original name but was invented by a local man with a view to capturing the attention of the tourists beginning to arrive on the island in numbers as road and rail access was improved.

The true name is Llanfair Pwllgwyngyll, as it appears on the road sign at the entrance to the village – the church of St Mary at Pwllgwyngyll – to distinguish its situation from any other of the many churches dedicated to the Virgin Mary. Although the Victorian building displays no evidence of the early history of the site, it does have one attractive modern stained glass window, recently installed, recalling the association of the parish with the 'Indefatigable' School whose boys attended church regularly when the school existed at Plas Llanfair, a mansion nearby. Now a Ministry of Defence self-catering holiday complex known as a Joint Service Mountain Training Centre, the building was originally the home of Admiral Lord Clarence Paget. After his death in 1898 it had several owners, at one time the Haigh-Wood family used it as a summer retreat. Their daughter, Vivienne, was the first wife of the poet T.S. Eliot.

The training establishment for boys, 'Indefatigable', began its existence in a 50-gun frigate anchored in the Mersey until 1912, when the ship was condemned, and the school moved to another ship at Rock Ferry on the Wirral, finding its final home at Plas Llanfair during the second world war, where it remained until 1995 when rising costs and a dwindling mercantile fleet put paid to any further activity. The window in the parish church recalls the development of the school from the beginning.

Two features of Llanfair Pwllgwyngyll stand side by side at the junction of the A5 and the road to Brynsiencyn. The octagonal toll house still carries a list of tolls high above its front door, money which had to be paid to allow admission through the road gate to the next section of the highway, until all road tolls were abolished. This is now a private house and a listed building.

Abutting it is the one-storey Women's Institute Hall which proudly displays a notice to say that the Llanfair Pwllgwyngyll Women's Institute was the first to be set up in Britain, in 1915. It met originally in an outbuilding of a private house in the village. The corrugated iron building near the toll house is kept in good repair. It is a first world war army hut from the Kinmel camp on the North Wales coast, erected here in 1921. The W.I. movement in Britain was instigated by a man, Colonel the Hon. Henry Stapleton-Cotton, whose belief in the capabilities of women to lead a busy and useful life led him to prompt its foundation. He lived close to Plas Newydd on the Brynsiencyn road. Among his other developments were a bacon factory and egg distribution centre near to the railway station, and a bulb and chicory farm.

The railway had the effect of opening up Anglesey still more, and the village developed further, close to the railway station.

Central in the village, opposite the War Memorial, stands Tŷ Coch. A plaque set in the garden wall reminds passers-by that this was the home of a famous Welshman, Sir John Morris-Jones, one of Wales's foremost Welsh

14

language scholars. He occupied the chair of Welsh at the University of Wales at Bangor and his great contribution to the renaissance of the Welsh language in the early years of the twentieth century was his Welsh Grammar, a volume of five hundred pages. He also edited cultural journals, was fascinated by old manuscripts, fine printing and calligraphy, and translated *Omar Khayam* into Welsh from the original Persian. In his more relaxed moments he enjoyed art, music and working with metal.

The newest development which has brought many visitors to Llanfair Pwllgwyngyll is the spacious department store standing alongside the railway line next to the station.

It was opened by the Scottish knitwear firm of James Pringle, but now belongs to Edinburgh Woollen Mills. The centre attracts many hundreds of browsers and shoppers throughout the year, many on their way to board the ferry to take them from Holyhead to Ireland. The local Tourist Information Centre at the entrance to the store is one of the busiest on the island.

Brynsiencyn

At first sight the village of Brynsiencyn might appear to be merely a bunch of insignificant houses where the A4080 makes a right angled turn away from the Menai Strait, on its way to Newborough. The cottages along the main street have received a face lift in recent years, which, although tidying the village, has resulted in a conformity which does away with individuality.

During the late 1800s and the early part of the 20th century this was a quarry-workers' village. Men made the ferry crossing to Felinheli, where they would be met by quarry wagons to transport them to the Dinorwig quarries above Llanberis. Here they would work for the week, sleeping in purpose-built accommodation on site, and return to their families at the weekend.

Quarry-workers were not the only ferry passengers. Before the bridges were built across the Menai Strait this was the mode of transport used by farmers from the west of Anglesey to take their produce to Caernarfon market, and by other country dwellers needing the amenities a sizeable town could offer.

The first passenger ferry service sailed across the mile-wide channel from Tal y Foel to Caernarfon in 1425. It could be a hazardous crossing, depending on weather and tides. The landing facilities on the Anglesey shore were so poor that, before a jetty was built, passengers had to be carried ashore on the backs of the ferrymen. The road down to the shore at Barras leaves the A4080 where the main road turns into the village opposite the car park.

At the approach to Brynsiencyn from Llanfair Pwllgwyngyll stands the parish church, built in 1846, its top-heavy square tower a landmark.

The original parish church of Llanidan, now ruined, was abandoned in 1843. It can be seen down a narrow lane hidden by trees four hundred metres from the Strait, south east of the village. Llanidan dates from the 14th century. The site is said to have been a religious one during the early 7th century, when Saint Nidan worshipped there. The 14th century building was double-aisled. It was associated originally with the convent in Beddgelert. A wall niche contained a reliquary of gritstone which, according to Giraldus Cambrensis in the 12th century, had . the mysterious power of 'being constant in one place'. If moved, it returned the same night – nobody knew how.

In his *Cambrian Travellers Guide* of 1808, the author Nicholson wrote 'Hugh Lupus, earl of Chester, determined to subdue its locomotive faculties, fastened it with a chain to a far greater stone and flung it into the sea, but to the astonishment of all beholders it was found next morning in its usual place. It is certainly now well secured for it forms a part of the wall of the church'. Of such legends are fantasies made!

The church at Llanidan was partly demolished when the stones were used in the fabric of the new church. The part which remained at Llanidan became a mortuary chapel. Some of the fittings – the bells, an oak chair and the font – were moved to the new building.

The new church was described by a contemporary writer as 'a debased and barbarous style, being neither architectural science nor taste'. Because of its similarity to St George's church, Llandudno, some attribute the design to the architect James Welch.

The large stone chapel in the centre of Brynsiencyn was once the spiritual home of a famous Welsh preacher, the Rev. John Williams. During the early years of the twentieth century he relinquished the pastorate to concentrate on his preaching, being in great demand throughout Wales for his oratory. He also channelled his efforts during the first world war to urging young men to enlist in the Forces to fight for their country, a move which brought him into disfavour with many Nonconformists who, until then, had been his fervent admirers and supporters.

The shore of the Menai Strait near to the village is claimed to have been the place where a battle was fought in 1157 when the Welsh were victorious over an army of Henry II. Nearby, too, the Romans are said to have attempted a landing but being met by a horde of wild-looking men and women with painted faces, screaming and brandishing weapons, they decided it was prudent to return to Segontium, their fort in what is now Caernarfon, and make other plans. Bearing in mind the so-called valour and fighting spirit which enabled the Romans to conquer so much of western Europe, this is hard to credit!

History around Brynsiencyn goes back even farther than Roman times, as several remains around the village testify. Castell Bryngwyn, a circular earthwork, has been excavated, the finds proving that there was settlement here from Neolithic times to the first century A.D. Caer

Leb is a site where Roman pottery has been found, but archaeologists believe it likely that its use as a settlement is much older. Both sites are to the west of the village.

This corner of Anglesey has nurtured its personalities, none more remarkable than Henry Rowlands, who became vicar of Llanidan in 1696. He was born in 1655 at Llanedwen, was ordained deacon at Bangor when he was twenty seven years old, and served the church for the rest of his life in this south west area of the island. He and his wife had twelve children.

As well as his work as a cleric, Henry Rowlands had wider interests. He was a historian, an amateur archeologist, and what might be termed today an environmentalist. Living in an agricultural community he felt that proper use should be made of the land. Until his day nobody had studied Anglesey as thoroughly as he did. In 1704 he published some of his findings in an essay on agriculture which laid emphasis on the importance of good husbandry. Shelter for animals in the windy countryside could be provided by planting more trees, building walls and fences. Home made fertilisers made of sand and rotted sea-shells, all found in abundance locally, could make for vast improvements in crops, he recommended.

In 1710 another work followed, this time dealing with local antiquities and the parishes in his own area.

He had made a friend of Edward Lhuyd, the botanist, who invited Rowlands along with other clergymen elsewhere in Britain to provide information on a number of topics relating to their own parishes, including the geography and natural history. It is not known how Henry Rowlands came to know the botanist, as he never visited

England, unless Lhuyd's repute had travelled to this remote corner of Wales as a result of his essays.

Keeping a watchful eye on five parishes, Henry Rowlands was able to supply the answer to Lhuyd's exhaustive queries.

Time and experience has proved some of his assertions to be incorrect, but nevertheless his writings provide readers today with a glimpse of what life must have been like in his own parishes during the early 18th century. Henry Rowlands died in 1723 and is buried in Llanedwen churchyard.

A little over two hundred years after Henry Rowlands was born in Llanedwen, Ellis Jones Griffiths was born in Birmingham. He was the son of a successful Welsh builder who retired early after making his fortune, and brought his family to live in Brynsiencyn.

Young Ellis was one of the first students to attend the new University of Wales at Aberystwyth, where he became interested in politics. From there he went on to Cambridge on a scholarship to study law. He was elected President of the Union in 1886, the first Welshman to attain the honour, where he was popular for his easy fluency in public speaking.

In 1893 he won the Parliamentary seat for the Liberals in Anglesey. His political activity was far-reaching. He worked incessantly for the disestablishment of the church in Wales. Overseas problems interested him. He supported the political rights of the coloured population of South Africa, one of the few who did so at that time, and he was in favour of votes for women in Britain.

In 1914 he became a member of the Privy Council and when knighted in 1918 changed his name to Ellis Jones

Ellis-Griffiths. After resigning from the Cabinet in 1915 he led a busy life as a barrister on law circuits in Chester and north and south Wales. He lost the Anglesey seat in 1918 to the Labour candidate, but served for a short time as Member for Carmarthen.

Sir Ellis Jones Ellis-Griffiths died while on circuit in south Wales in 1926 and is buried at Llanidan churchyard, Brynsiencyn.

Many visitors to Anglesey make for the Sea Zoo at Brynsiencyn, near to the Mermaid Inn on the shore road. There are directional signs from all approaches to the village. This is rightly held to be one of Anglesey's most popular tourist attractions where great emphasis is placed on environmental issues concerning the coastal water of the Menai Strait.

Two ex-Bangor university graduates, David and Alison Lea-Wilson, settled here as oyster farmers and fish merchants. In 1983 they took on a partner and set up the Anglesey Sea Zoo, developing their common interests in marine biology and handling live oysters and lobsters before selling on the open market. One thing led to another, and more money was invested. David and Alison Lea-Wilson eventually bought out their partner and channelled their energies and resources into this unique complex to develop still further. Now thousands of visitors each year come for an insight into this life of the sea. Tanks are fed with sea water from the Strait. The aim is to give a picture of off-shore life as it would be seen if one could dive below and view for oneself.

The Zoo remains open for most of the year. It has a reputation for being upgraded regularly with conservation and breeding projects high on the list of priorities.

Brynsiencyn is one of the places in Anglesey which boasts a new industry, thanks to David and Alison Lea-Wilson. They have diversified successfully by establishing Cwmni Halen Môr Môn – Anglesey Sea Salt Company.

Salt is harvested from the water around Anglesey, the process resulting in high quality white-flaked salt.

Demand soon promised to outstrip production as the new product found favour with gourmets throughout Britain. It is possible to buy Halen Môr Môn through a variety of outlets from specialist delicatessen shops to famous London department stores, and the demand is still growing.

At present, seven are employed in this industry.

Menter Môn, a business development agency, publishes graphic leaflets on the attractions of south west Anglesey, in *Natural Attractions on the Isle of Anglesey*, *Historic Anglesey* and a walkers guide to the Brynsiencyn area which is one of four in the *Walk with the Saints on the Isle of Anglesey* series. These are available at Tourist Information Centres, libraries and at some hotels. Anglesey Sea Zoo publishes its own informative leaflets on the Zoo and Halen Môr Môn.

Newborough

The village of Newborough, grouped around a meeting of roads where once stood a cross and stocks, comes into its own in the summer when hordes of visitors drive their cars down the road signposted 'Llanddwyn beach' to the wide stretch of sand beyond the dunes. Some, with an enquiring mind, ask why the village has an English name in a part of Anglesey which otherwise appears to be essentially Welsh. The answer lies in its connection with the village of Llanfaes and the town of Beaumaris on the eastern coast of Anglesey.

Originally called Rhosyr, what is now Newborough was given its name by Edward I when he created a new settlement here in 1303, moving nearly all the population of Llanfaes to enable him to build Beaumaris castle near there. The newly created 'borough' became famous for its markets and fairs. Before Thomas Telford built his road across the island early in the 19th century Newborough was on one of the chief routes for travellers and farmers who wished to cross the Menai Strait from Anglesey to Caernarfon.

A writer to the journal *Cymru* in 1902 described how people would dress in their best to attend the fairs in holiday mood. He added, 'if Newborough is without handsome buildings, great riches and the busy trade of

Birmingham and Liverpool, it has history'.

The history to which he referred is evident today on the edge of the village, where a recent archaeological dig has uncovered the site of considerable size near the parish church, the foundations of one of the principal courts of the medieval Welsh princes. This is now open for all to see.

The court site was covered by sand over six hundred years ago when one hundred and eighty three acres of the borough lands were overwhelmed by sea and sand during a succession of storms which also destroyed eleven cottages. These dwellings, called 'Hendai', have now been excavated from the sand and can be seen by walkers using one of the forest trails.

The land around and to the south of Newborough, now known as Newborough Warren and Newborough Forest, is one of the largest dune areas in Britain. The forest came into being during 1948 when Corsican Pine, other conifers and some deciduous trees were planted to prevent sand being blown on to the roads and the agricultural land nearby.

Following the great storms of the 14th century laws were passed in the time of Elizabeth I to forbid the destruction of marram grass, as it was recognised how this stabilised the dunes and prevented the movement of sand on the Warren. Today, Newborough Warren is a national nature reserve. The information centre at the car park open to visitors near the entrance to Llanddwyn beach during the summer explains the aims of the conservancy and the forestry. Various trails cross the forest and the warren, popular with bird watchers and nature lovers.

In its heyday Newborough Warren provided a means

of livelihood for the inhabitants of Newborough, who snared rabbits. It was estimated up to one hundred thousand rabbits a year were caught, but this number has dwindled because of tree planting and the plague of myxamatosis in 1954, although there are still plenty to be seen. The Warren can be explored from the car park at Pen Lôn, reached by turning with the sign at the roundabout before reaching the village from the Menai Strait direction.

There is a grassy path leading from the car park, along a static dune surface. Wet 'slacks' (pools of water) are scattered in between the dunes and those with an eye for such things will recognise a variety of plants which can flourish in such surroundings. Nearer to the sea the dunes shift with the wind and plants find it difficult to survive. Various species of birds and other wild life abound, and some of these may be seen from the hide on the edge of Llyn Rhos Ddu near to the car park.

Another industry which flourished at one time in Newborough was mat-making, where local people worked in their homes, using the grass they had collected from the dunes to plait mats and haystack covers for use on the farms as well as using it to make brushes for whitewashing their buildings.

Women and girls gathered the marram grass during the summer, dried it and stored it behind the cottages. Villagers were allowed to rent plots where the grass was grown specifically for use. The cut marram was left in conical sheaves to dry in the air, in a similar way to corn sheaves once stacked in the fields. They ripened here for three weeks, then the ripened stems were shaken out to remove any seeds and sand, made into sheaves once more, and thatched roughly with the stubble to be left until they could be carted conveniently back to the village, ready for storing and plaiting.

The stems were plaited together to make long 'laces', a number of these being sewn together to make mats of the required width and length. An eighty-metres length was long enough to cover a haystack.

Women bartered the mats at local shops or, if they worked for a farmer, were paid according to what they could produce.

The craft was organised as a co-operative industry in 1913, when Colonel Stapleton-Cotton of Llanfair Pwllgwyngyll, who was later to set in motion the nationwide Women's Institute movement, set up the Newborough Mat Makers Association, which enabled the industry to work on a more businesslike basis. It ended the barter system and new buyers from farther afield were found which meant that there was enough work to carry the industry along successfully to meet changing needs. Ropes, baskets, and table mats were also made. The industry survived in this way until the 1930's.

The marram grass industry was women's work. Many men took to the sea, and were often away for months at a time. One elderly Newborough resident recalls her grandmother saying that children in the village were often known by their mother's name rather than by their father's, as fathers were so often at sea for such long periods that their appearances at home were spasmodic.

Newborough could claim its fair share of sea captains, of men whose work was associated with the sea and who developed other spheres of interest as a result. Captain William Jones was one. He became a shipping and estate agent, a property developer, a mining entrepreneur and a civic leader in Australia in the 19th century.

The large half-timbered building standing on a slight rise in the village is the Prichard-Jones Institute, fronted by six attractive almshouses.

Sir John Prichard-Jones was a native of Newborough. Born into a working-class farming family, he left the local school at the age of fourteen and was apprenticed to a store in Caernarfon to learn the drapery trade.

John Prichard-Jones later worked in several English towns before joining the staff of Dickens' Regent Street shop in London in 1874, where he eventually became a director and chairman of the company now known as Dickens & Jones. Among other public offices he held were those of Sheriff of Anglesey (in 1905), treasurer of the Welsh National Museum, and a member of the Council of the North Wales University College at Bangor and Vice President of the Council. His name is perpetuated in the University's large concert hall, and his coat of arms appears with those of the City of London, the University of Wales, and the county of Anglesey, above the door to the Hall.

Prichard-Jones maintained his association with the south-eastern corner of Anglesey, having a country house at Dwyran, the next village to Newborough. During his lifetime he would have heard of a community building being erected in Cemaes Bay, the gift of local philanthropist, David Hughes, which may have planted the seed of an idea in his own mind when he determined to give a similar facility to Newborough. He lived in an age of philanthropy, when many ordinary people who had made good in commerce sought to benefit the communities from which they had sprung.

The foundation stone of the Prichard-Jones Institute was laid on August 26, 1902, an occasion when Newborough turned out in its best clothes for the grand event. Prichard-Jones's vision was far-seeing and generous. He planned to provide a library, public hall, coffee room, reading room, smoking room and other offices for the use of the residents of the almshouses and the people of the village and outlying districts.

Those eligible to be residents in the houses had to be 'married couples of good report who must have been residents within the parish of Newborough for at least ten years, or must have lived in the parish for not less than ten years before the date of application'.

The same rule applied to single applicants. No male was considered for residence who was under sixty-five years of age, and no female under fifty-five.

There were further restrictions. Those not eligible were married persons with young children, 'professional paupers', 'persons convicted of felony or misdemeanors; persons of notoriously bad character'. No religious services were allowed in the Hall, but every resident had to attend a place of worship for at least one service a week if he or she was physically and mentally fit to do so. Alcohol and gambling were prohibited. Residents were expected to keep their own houses clean and tidy and also to take their share of the work of maintaining the Institute and grounds.

There were strict rules for those occupying the houses – for instance, 'earth closet pans supplied to the Institute and to each of the six cottages are to be emptied daily and the contents thereof are to be placed upon the respective garden plots and are to be dug into the earth'.

When the complex was opened, residents had a pension of five shillings a week. Four of the six houses grouped charmingly around a central garden were for single occupants and two for couples. The cost at the beginning of the twentieth century was expected to be about £6,000 and Prichard-Jones invested £7,000 extra to meet the cost of running the Institute, the wages of the overseer, books and papers for the library, pensions, etc.

Today the Prichard-Jones charity is run by a trust. At its centenary the Grade II* listed building and the cottages are the subject of conservation and restoration to bring them up to present day standards, costing in the region of £750,000.

Due to lack of foresight by earlier trustees, following the destruction of properties in London during air raids, rents from which had provided money for the maintenance and running of the Newborough Institute, the land in the city was not sold. Now, when money is needed urgently, income has to be used carefully, but an application for Heritage Lottery money is pending.

All the activities of a busy village take place here. Further education classes meet and the library is well used. The cottages still provide homes for a succession of elderly residents who, although they no longer receive a pension from the charity, pay only small rents as costs are well subsidised.

If Lottery money is allocated and the Trust continues to work conscientiously, the aims of Sir John Prichard-Jones will continue well into the future.

Malltraeth

Writing in *Anglesey and the North Wales Coast Book*, in the 1960s, Henry Glazebrook commented . . .

To see the little hamlet of Malltraeth yard dreaming on the edge of the Cefni Marshes one would suppose that nothing ever happened here; nothing, that is to say, beyond the quiet tilling of the fields and the patient fishing of its tidal waters. Yet in the past this locality has from time to time been the scene of great activity.

There was a time when the Cefni river was tidal almost as far inland as Llangefni, twelve miles from the coast. It is difficult to imagine today as the river is channelled between raised banks and sheep graze on the reclaimed land to each side.

In earlier times there were two river crossings, one from the hamlet of Malltraeth which was marked by a large black stone. The cottage, Rhyd y Maen Du, later marked the spot. In the days before Telford cut across Anglesey with his London-to-Holyhead road the way from Holyhead to the Menai Strait ferries to the west of the island took travellers across the Afon Cefni here, and this is also where drovers ushered their cattle over the river. The other crossing was farther inland, marked by a white stone.

Angharad Llwyd who wrote a winning essay in 1832 which she titled *Island of Mona* described Malltraeth Marsh as 'a tract of enclosed and cultivated land three miles long and two and a half miles in breadth, besides two miles long and one broad of marshland', adding that 'the waste land called Malltraeth or Sandy Marsh is supposed to be six miles in length, belonging to different parishes adjoining'.

Over a number of years, during the 18th century, there was much discussion about draining the marsh, but costs were prohibitive. After two abortive efforts to put work in hand, an Act of Parliament in 1790 initiated work to drain the land, the cost to be met by the various landowners who would benefit eventually by the extra useful farmland it would make available to them. To do this effectively it was necessary to build a cob (dyke) to keep out the high tides which were a constant menace to any conservation.

An embankment of furze faggots was planned, bound with cordage and covered with sand and sods. This was to be 1280 metres long; 46 metres wide at the base, tapering to 3.7 metres wide; and 4.6 metres high. Work began at both ends at the same time, the two halves to be joined in the middle. This middle section was the most difficult to complete, as this is where the water was most forceful. Costs were high. There were unpredictable difficulties in construction and in 1796 an unusually high tide breached the embankment, halting the work.

Nothing more was attempted until 1811 when yet another Act of Parliament was passed to make available more money from the landowners, and the work was completed eventually at a cost of around £50,000, an enormous sum in those days.

During the completion the centre gap was plugged with an old hulk, towed from Caernarfon and filled with rubble. It remains in the cob foundations to this day.

A road was built alongside the cob, from Malltraeth to Newborough, much to the relief of farmers who had so often experienced great difficulty in taking their cattle across the river. The Cefni was then channelled with the intention of making it navigable by small boats.

The effect of the new cob was felt in several ways. It eased the access to the Strait ferries from Holyhead, it facilitated the removal of coal from the small mines a mile or two up river, and allowed it to be loaded conveniently on to ships at Malltraeth. The copper industry at Mynydd Parys was developing fast, and the coal dug on the marsh supplied a need at Amlwch without being too costly to transport. And, of course, the road improved intercourse between neighbouring districts. As a result Malltraeth began to develop from a tiny hamlet to a village.

In *Hanes Plwyf Trefdraeth*, the Rev. O. Hughes, rector of Trefdraeth in 1900, quoted population figures. In 1811, he claimed, 497 lived in the parish which included Malltraeth. By 1881 this figure had risen to 894, but dropped by 1901 to 692 as it felt the effect of the general migration from the country to the cities where work was more plentiful, and the closure of the coal mines near Pentre Berw.

By today industry, except for farming, has forsaken the village which had experienced comparative prosperity following the building of the cob. Malltraeth is now the haunt of holidaymakers and day visitors who come to take a walk along the ridge of the embankment to enjoy the air and to watch the many birds who alight on the brackish pools between the cob and the road.

The proliferation of birds was to tempt artist Charles Tunnicliffe to make his home in a house called Shorelands whose larger picture window looks out south west on to the s-bend of the river Cefni as it flows to the sea. When the tide is high a wall is all that separates the mile-wide estuary from the garden.

Charles Tunnicliffe came to live in Malltraeth in 1947, aged forty-six. He had been brought up in the Cheshire border foothills, spending holidays in Anglesey. In all he illustrated eighty eight country books, but he is even better known for his brilliant studies of birds, many of them drawn and painted as he sat by his studio window at Shorelands looking out across the water. They reflected the intense study he made of their plumage and behaviour. Tunnicliffe is regarded as one of the foremost exponents of wildlife in Britain during the 20th century.

A replica of his studio has been set up at Oriel Ynys Môn in Llangefni, the gallery which houses a comprehensive collection of his work.

Malltraeth does not have a parish church, but a missionary chapel under the direction of the Trefdraeth parish was begun in the schoolroom built in the village in 1870, and which is still used for village worship. Regular services were held under a lay reader and it proved very successful. Seating eighty, it was almost full every Sunday, and had a Sunday school of upwards of fifty.

Aberffraw

The visitor to the small village of Aberffraw at the beginning of the present century finds it difficult to appreciate the activity which took place there in earlier times. Aberffraw is linked to Celtic mythology, to early Welsh government and jurisdiction, to the days when its fairs and markets drew the population of the surrounding countryside to its village square, and to its thriving small shipbuilding industry.

Today Aberffraw is a cluster of houses, church and chapels, squatting quietly and comfortably above the high water-mark of the tidal River Ffraw which rises only a short distance away in Llyn Coron and flows through sandy banks to the estuary in Aberffraw Bay.

The attractive, ancient bridge which has appeared on many camera shots, is now by-passed by a modern concrete crossing. One can wait in Bodorgan Square on a hot summer's day for the local bus and meet no-one. Cars parked near the bridge, among the sand dunes on the far side of the river, may have brought visitors but they make their way with their picnic baskets and sun hats along the river to the estuary and the wide sands of Traeth Mawr to search for fresh air, sea breezes, a bathe and a sun tan. Or they wander across the dunes where their voices are suddenly muted. And so Aberffraw is left to itself, with only the gulls for visitors.

The western coast of Anglesey is rich in early history. There are traces of occupation – the Din Dryfol burial chamber near to Aberffraw, a tumulus and hut groups vouch for the fact that men hunted, camped and died here. Mesolithic flints and implements have been excavated within the last fifty years at Trwyn Du. These are partly finished and broken blades, cores and nodules said to be the waste material from making barbs and points for harpoons and arrows, found in and near a Bronze Age barrow.

In 1777 an estate survey commented 'Hereabout anciently stood the Royal Palace of the Princes of Wales of Welsh Blood of which at Present Nothing remains – the stone having been carried for making Hedges and for buildings houses about thirty years ago'.

When Lewis compiled his *Topographical Dictionary of Wales* in 1833 he described Aberffraw as having 'a small harbour capable of receiving vessels of forty tons burden . . . anciently an excellent haven . . . Great quantities of grain (oats and barley) raised in the parish and surrounding country are annually shipped from this small port which is considered a creek within the limits of the port of Beaumaris. The inhabitants are principally employed in agriculture and fishing'.

A list of the harbours of Wales compiled during the reign of Edward VI includes Aberffraw. Vessels built at the port in early days were used for fishing and coastal trade and later the need for transporting goods from the copper industry at Mynydd Parys stimulated the building and re-building of ships.

Every port in Anglesey had its characters associated

with the sea and ships. Robert Beaver, born in Aberffraw in 1748, was one of these. He went to sea as a very young man and was soon commanding his own ship and involved in foreign trading. These were the days of the slave trade when fortunes could be made, and Robert Beaver was not one for missing an opportunity. He traded with the African west coast ports, where he exchanged his shipments of linens and woollens for cargoes of slaves, trading them in the West Indies for cotton and sugar which he brought back to England. Eventually he owned the largest privateer in the West Indies, amassing a fortune by capturing over fifty prizes on the high seas. But poor health finally forced him to return home.

Robert Beaver settled with his wife and large family of eleven children in Amlwch, where he undertook voluntarily responsibility for the Point Lynas light and pilot service on the north-eastern tip of the island. This was before the present lighthouse was built, and the light and the pilot station were in a farmhouse, the light being two oil lamps with small metal reflectors set into a tower. Robert Beaver died in Amlwch about 1812.

Another association with the sea existed on Anglesey's west coast, when looting a shipwreck was considered a crime by society, yet daring by those who lived in the Aberffraw area where the temptation from the high number of shipwrecks was too great. In 1823 the ship *Flora* was lost with all hands, and two Aberffraw men were sentenced to six months in prison for stealing from the wreck. When released they were publicly flogged at Aberffraw, where a large crowd gathered to watch.

The importance of Aberffraw as a trading centre can be assessed from the fact that six fairs were held each year.

There were few shops in Anglesey before the end of the 18th century although Aberffraw boasted two – a grocery shop and another which sold 'articles of all kinds'. The cattle fair and the markets survived until 1812, by which time Llangefni had become the centre of commercial activity.

The district had its own unique postal service in the mid-19th century. Soon after 1840 when the penny post was introduced the postmaster would stand in his doorway when the mailbag arrived and call out the names of the addressees. A small group of women and young boys would be waiting to carry the letters to remote farms, the recipients paying them for doing so.

For centuries before Sir Arthur Owen of Bodowen built his picturesque bridge over the River Ffraw in 1731, the crossing by people and cattle had to be made by wading across further upstream.

His bridge, now by-passed, is one of the most attractively-designed in Anglesey and carries the date for all to see. In 1871 it passed into the ownership of the Bodorgan estate. The long, steep approaches meet in a hog's back on top of the bridge. It was built of dry random and rubble stone-work with the single arch roughly dressed. The workmanship shows the skill of local craftsmen.

The narrow roadway became unsuitable for modern traffic, so a new bridge was planned as part of a road improvement scheme in the area in the 1930s. It was to be the closing link in an eight mile stretch of road between Aberffraw and Rhosneigr, connecting with the main A5 at Treban.

The new bridge was opened in May 1932 by Major Sir

George Ll.T.G. Meyrick of Bodorgan and Lady Meyrick. Its erection had posed a problem as the land close to the old bridge and upstream was shifting sand. Eventually engineers decided upon 121 pre-cast concrete piles driven into the earth in groups of three, connected at the top with reinforced concrete caps. It is this structure which carries today's traffic.

The parish church at Aberffraw is a mixture of styles, as additions have been made over the centuries. There are 12th century traces but the main additions were made from the 16th century onwards. Two copper collecting shovels with thick wooden handles are dated 1777, and the plate includes a silver paten of 1753. The font is medieval.

Sir Arthur Owen, who built the first bridge, also repaired an old ruin called Eglwys y Beili in 1729, intending it as a school which he endowed with £4 a year. Angharad Llwyd, writing her history of Anglesey, further comments 'very sensibly prohibiting all foreign languages' (referring, we presume, to English and Latin), 'thereby ensuring to the six poor children a knowledge of the scriptures (as wisely enacted by the rubric) in the vulgar tongue'.

The future of the Llys Llywelyn Countryside Centre in Aberffraw, housed in an attractive cluster of one-storey stone buildings in the centre of the village, hangs in the balance at the time of writing. This was opened in May, 1988, as a tourist attraction, to highlight the history and environment of the area. It displayed a number of information panels, a large fish tank, tactile exhibits, an audio visual show; and a gift shop and children's play room as well as a small cafe added to the attractions. It has been proposed that the Centre be converted into a field study centre where certain facilities will also be available to the local community, and it may also provide accommodation for tourists intending to walk the coastal footpath.

Rhosneigr

Rhosneigr is an Anglesey village which has grown from a cluster of cottages and a coastguard station into a popular small seaside resort in a little over one hundred years, thanks to the early twentieth century fashion for taking summer holidays away from the bustle of the towns and cities of the north west of England.

It is a village built on sand dunes. Large Edwardian houses, built by affluent industrialists and merchants whose families would spend weeks here at a time, stand alongside bungalows and more modern – and modest – estates. There is the occasional reminder of village housing before development, with the more traditional cottages and chapels.

Perfect beaches for swimming; safety for children to paddle or build their sand castles; conditions ideal for wind-surfing or horse-riding; an excellent golf course; the opportunity to fish. Rhosneigr has them all.

In the 18th century this was a remote and desolate area of sand dunes, wind-blown in winter. Glorious summer weather now attracts holiday makers to the two broad sandy beaches of Traeth Llydan and Traeth Cymyran, but storms at any time of the year create high seas which lash these western shores of Anglesey remorselessly and turn oaradise into a place fraught with danger. In the days of sail many ships were wrecked. The sea bed is littered with rotting hulks and there are countless stories of heroic rescues. Many stories, too, of smugglers and land-based 'pirates' called *Lladron Crigyll* (Crigyll Murderers) who would lure unsuspecting ships to their doom on the rocks by hanging lighted lanterns around the necks of cattle to simulate undulating ships' lights in harbour. This was a practice rife in Cornwall, called Cornish Lamping. When ships had been lured on to the rocks the perpetrators would plunder.

Lewis Morris, customs officer at Holyhead, reported to the Admiralty in 1741 that 'false charts serve but as false lights laid by villains along ye coast to lead poor sailors to destruction'.

One of the most famous shipwrecks to take place off Rhosneigr was that of the *Norman Court* which sank in Cymyran Bay in March 1883.

The barque was bound for Greenock with a cargo of sugar from Java when it was driven ashore by a strong gale. Two of the twenty-two crew died after a night spent in the rigging. The crews of Rhosneigr and Holyhead lifeboats went to the rescue but three attempts in two hours failed. Experienced seamen from Holyhead were put on a special train from Holyhead to Rhosneigr, and they went out in the Rhosneigr lifeboat. They managed to rescue all the survivors. The Holyhead men received R.N.L.I. awards in recognition of their persistence and bravery.

The main road (A4080) into Rhosneigr makes a wide detour around the village, encompassing Llyn Maelog lying between the railway and the sea. The church at Llanfaelog, the parish church for Rhosneigr, stands on a rise overlooking the railway and the lake. A cell was founded here by Saint Maelog in AD 605. The church was re-built entirely in the 19th century on a new site in the existing churchyard. Some of the fittings from the previous church have been included.

Not all in Rhosneigr is comparatively new, however. There are the remains of two burial chambers within the parish – Pentre Traeth and Tŷ Newydd. Tŷ Newydd was excavated in 1935 but little of interest was found there. There is also an early sixth century inscribed standing stone.

Llyn Maelog is one of the largest of Anglesey's lakes in this western part of the island. It is a favourite place with bird-watchers and botanists who come searching for birds and rare and common plants found in this special environment.

Visitors staying at the Maelog Lake Hotel have the best of both worlds – views over Traeth Llydan into the sunset (and sunsets really are a feature on this west-facing coastline) – and over Llyn Maelog across the greensward of the Anglesey Golf Club.

The hotel has a story to tell. It was built in 1863 as Rhosneigr began to be popular with tourists, the brain-child of Evan Thomas, one of the famous bone-setter family from Anglesey who had gone to live and practise in Liverpool. Evan Thomas had bought the rights to the common from the Department of Woods and Forests, and the land had until then been used openly by local people for grazing their animals. When news came of the intention to build, they considered those rights were usurped in spite of Evan Thomas's promise to the contrary.

The 1860s saw a strong temperance revival in Anglesey. This fuelled objections to a hotel where strong drink would be served. Feelings ran so high that Evan Thomas was forced to employ a guard on the site each night to be alert to any move on the part of the objectors. Events reached a climax in October 1863, when a crowd attacked the guard, threw him into the lake, and blew up part of the newly built hotel. The miscreants were brought to justice at Beaumaris Crown Court and gaoled.

The new hotel did much to attract a new type of visitor to Rhosneigr, those who enjoyed fishing in the lake. Artists, too, flocked to the village to take advantage of the exceptionally clear light which is a feature of this coast.

Having found the area so attractive, some visitors built their own homes. George Cockram, the landscape painter who worked in the Conwy Valley and in Anglesey, built his house here in 1895 and remained in Rhosneigr until 1950 when he died tragically as a result of falling into a fire in his studio. Another house in the village was occupied by the parents of the pilot of the ill-fated airship, R101, who flew it over the village in 1930 so that his mother and the villagers could admire this wonderful new invention.

The railway station at Llanfaelog was built some years after the line had been laid across the island, in answer to the demand by tourism. The Maelog Lake Hotel, in the 1920s, advertised 'Motors meet all trains'.

The end of the 19th century was to see still more development plans in the vicinity of the village. The extensive area north west of Afon Crigyll, Tywyn Trewan, had been targeted by the Welsh Explosives Co. Ltd., as an ideal site for a factory. In 1897 an enquiry was held at a local hotel when those attending were told that the company sought permission to occupy fifty five acres of the common to build and operate a factory to manufacture and store gelignite under the 1875 Explosives Act. The company had received approval from the Home Office to manufacture, but the purpose of the enquiry was said 'simply to decide whether the site on which we propose to erect this factory is a suitable site'. The applicants claimed there would be work for three hundred, and the industry would also create other work opportunities as spin-offs.

But by this time tourism had become important to Rhosneigr.

One objector to the scheme voiced the opinion of the majority at the meeting when he said 'Rhosneigr is the most rising watering place in Anglesey and to have a dynamite factory erected within a mile of the place will be absolute ruin'. Objections were so numerous and so fierce that the development never took place.

Tywyn Trewan remained a wilderness for nearly half a century before any other attempt was made to invade it. This 1400 acre common land was partially encroached eventually, when three local businessmen laid out part of it as Anglesey Golf Club in 1914, again to attract tourists, but it was not until the second world war, in 1941, that R.A.F. Rhosneigr, soon to become known as R.A.F. Valley, was deemed a suitable development which would not impinge on tourism in the area.

R.A.F. Rhosneigr was opened as a Sector Operations Centre for the control of fighter defence in the approaches to Merseyside and Belfast, as well as a protection for shipping in the Irish Sea. At first, sand blown on to the airfield from the dunes of Traeth Cymyran by prevailing westerly winds caused severe problems to aircraft engines. This was eventually resolved by the dumping of tons of mud dredged from the nearby lakes, Llyn Penrhyn and Llyn Traffwll.

Towards the end of the war, R.A.F. Valley was used by the U.S. Army Air Force Transit Unit. In 1948 it became a permanent R.A.F. station when night flying training began. No.4 Flying Training School was based here, where instructors were taught how to instruct, and the station also housed the Search and Rescue Training Unit and the R.A.F. Valley Mountain Rescue Team.

In these early years of the twenty-first century Rhosneigr still charms those looking for sea-side relaxation and the proximity of a well-used airfield seems to be an added attraction.

Pentre Berw, Gwalchmai and Bryngwran

Industry was once the main feature of the tiny village of Pentre Berw which, today, is an adjunct to its near neighbour, Gaerwen. It stands on the hill above the reclaimed ground on the banks of the River Cefni.

The English name of Pentre Berw, Holland Arms, reflects the importance of the Holland family who once lived at Plas Berw, the ancient house below the road to Llangaffo. The first house, of which only ruins remain, was built by Ithel ap Howell around 1480. This was a single storey building with a central hall in between a solar and domestic offices. Around 1536 an upper floor was added and at the turn of that century, a square three-storey building attached to the solar. Sir Thomas Holland's house was of two storeys with attics and a slated roof.

Sir Thomas Holland was a wealthy man. Not only did he build the new Plas Berw but he maintained a town house in Beaumaris, and had a chapel erected for himself at his parish church of Llanidan. He prospected for coal at Llanfihangel Esceifiog in the Cefni valley. He had the right to fish for oysters in the Menai Strait.

Near to the house, which can be glimpsed across the marsh from the Holyhead road, stands an ivy-clad chimney, a remnant of the Cefni valley coal industry.

In 1812, long after the death of Sir Thomas Holland, three seams of coal were discovered on the Berw estate. The then owners, Lord Uxbridge and Berw Griffith, leased the pits to commercial companies. At that time coal was a very expensive item in Anglesey, far beyond the means of the working class, as it had to be carried from Liverpool and the cost of transporting it was high. Local people were encouraged to go to Berw to collect their own supplies. Some, with an eye to business and owning a suitable cart, collected for re-selling elsewhere at a profit. If they had no horse-drawn cart they would arrive with a mule and panniers.

Four tunnels were opened. Health and safety in the mines was non-existent, and the miners were lowered into the pits in a basket. Accidents were common. By 1861 the mines had ceased to produce, so the venture closed down, although in 1900 there was an outcry for the seams to be opened again but this did not happen.

The last of the Holland family to live at Plas Berw left money to the butler, on the condition that he opened a school for poor children. The bequest included a cottage and a plot of land. Schoolmasters kept these benefits until 1851 when they were transferred to the new school at Gaerwen.

The Welsh name, Pentre Berw, could possibly refer to a place where watercress grew. Or 'berw' might refer to the waterfall which cascades down the steep-sided rock in wet weather. Linguists are undecided.

Down the hill from Pentre Berw towards Holyhead the land becomes marshy, part of the Malltraeth Marsh (Cors Ddygau) created when the deep Cefni estuary was drained by building the Cob at Malltraeth. Where the tide once washed the land it is now crossed by two main roads, the A5 and the A55. Straight channels guide the river water and sheep graze on the reclaimed pasture.

Since the 19th century, plants have been sold on the site of the present Holland Arms Garden Centre. At first this was a nursery where plants were grown for sale. The business collapsed and the site remained derelict for a while until it was bought by the parents of the present owner, David Knock, in 1953 and converted into a Garden Centre when the fashion for such centres gained popularity in the 1970s.

Today David Knock proudly claims that even in an industry which is continually developing, Holland Arms Garden Centre is one of the most flourishing in north west Wales. An on-going programme of special events draws the crowds to the tiny village of Pentre Berw, and keeps between forty and fifty people in employment, depending on the season.

Across the road is a smaller nursery which specialises in the more unusual garden plants.

Continuing along Telford's Holyhead road, now forsaken by heavy and through traffic for the A55 expressway and given the status of a 'Heritage Route' indicated by the brown and cream sign of coach and horses, the traveller reaches Gwalchmai. The road passes through the outer fringe of the village, as the greater part lies to one side. Its name was originally Trewalchmai, explaining that it was the home of Gwalchmai ap Meilyr, court poet to Owain Gwynedd. He died in 1180. Writing in *The Island of Mona* Angharad Llwyd comments on the increase in population from 1821 to 1831, from 670 to 719, no doubt due in part to an improved road and maybe to

Llanfairpwll – The Toll House

Llanfairpwll – looking south to the Anglesey Column

Brynsiencyn – the turning to Newborough

The Prichard-Jones Institute
Newborough

Newborough: The remains of the court of the Princes, Rhosyr.

Malltraeth from the Cob

River Cefni at Malltraeth

Eglwys Berffro

Llys Llywelyn – Cofeb Jonah 1

Aberffraw reflections

Aberffraw – the village centre – Bodorgan Square

Pentre Berw; road-side cottages

Gwalchmai – a roadside hostelry

Capel Salem, Bryngwran

Y Ffynnon – Lôn Ffynnon, Bryngwran

Fali – where road and rail meet

Bodedern – London Road

The Stanley Pump, Bodedern

Llyn Traffwll in Anglesey's lake district

Llanddeusant – the church of Two Saints

Pont yr Arw chapel, Llanfachraeth; spiritual home of
Thomas Jesse Jones

Llanfechell – William Bulkeley's village

The Rev. James Williams's
church at Llanfairynghornwy

The David Hughes Village Hall
at Cemaes

A quiet morning at Cemaes

Waiting to sail at Cemaes

Llannerch y medd, the sleepy village centre

Redundant church,
Llannerch y medd

Plaque to "Llew Llwyfo"
at Penysarn

Plaque to Bedwyr Lewis Jones at Penysarn

Point Lynas, Llaneilian

Moelfre

The Panton Arms, Pentraeth, perpetuates the name of the
Panton family of Plas Gwyn

Ifor Thomas's memorial at Pentraeth.

Cottages at Llangoed

Cornelyn, Llangoed; the home of the botanical artists,
the Massey sisters

Llangoed – a small village street

increased activity in the nearby stone quarry.

The land around Gwalchmai is rocky. Gorse splashes colour over the outcrops. The narrower road encircling the village passes cottages which may well have been there in Angharad Llwyd's day, if not earlier. The church of St Morhaiarn stands in its quiet backwater, unprepossessing yet ancient. Experts say its date is uncertain but the north chapel was added c.1500 and the chancel and nave were rebuilt in 1674.

The octagonal tollhouse on the main road is a reminder of the days when travellers to and from Holyhead had to pay their dues before they were allowed through the gate to continue their journey to Caergeiliog or Llanfair Pwllgwyngyll tollgates.

Today's visitors know Gwalchmai for two reasons – the ever-popular Anglesey Show and the proximity of Mona airfield. Car drivers are likely to be stopped while low-flying aircraft land or take off, or perform their 'circuits and bumps'.

The Anglesey Showground to the other side of the A5 is peaceful enough for most of the year, but during the second week of August the picture is very different.

In the 1870s, when the present Anglesey Agricultural Society came into being, county agricultural societies were supported by landowners with the purpose of introducing their tenant farmers to new methods and up to date equipment, as well as encouraging rivalry and perfecting standards. The landowners hoped that the benefits gained might be reflected in local farming. These were the days when farms were smaller holdings of thirty to sixty acres and farmers made attempts to be self-sufficient. Corn was the chief crop, and cattle were reared for the English markets.

The first Anglesey Show to be organised by this new body was held in 1886 at Llannerch-y-medd. For the first years it was peripatetic, and expanded as new classes were introduced. Several shows were held on the Bodwina fields on the outskirts of Gwalchmai, and then on part of Mona airfield. Fringe attractions were added with the purpose of attracting families, a move decried by the more purist agriculturists. Anything to increase attendance as shows were becoming expensive to stage. By 1970 there were 170 stands, and Anglesey Show had become one of the most prestigious in Wales.

By 1973, attendance reached 31,000.

Ground rents had risen astronomically, and the committee decided that buying their own site would, in the end, be advantageous. The Glan Gors farm went on the market, and was snapped up by the Anglesey Agricultural Society. Buildings to house certain show sections have been erected on the site, which is now regarded as second to none in Wales.

Mona airfield has been in existence since the first world war, when the German U-boat campaign was launched in 1915.

In January 1915 three ships had been sunk by a U-boat in Liverpool Bay, and two more in February. The admiralty decided to fight this new threat with small airships which would patrol the sea between Wales and Ireland and in Liverpool Bay, to be based at Wigtown and Anglesey. A site on farmland near Gwalchmai was chosen, the land requisitioned, and so Mona airfield came into being. In the beginning it went by a variety of names, but eventually Llangefni Airfield was the popular choice – possibly because Llangefni was easier to pronounce than

Gwalchmai! Later still, the name of Mona was adopted.

Preparation of the site brought employment to the island. A large airship shed was necessary to house four airships, as well as workshops, a gas plant and gasholders and huts for personnel.

When fully manned, 130-150 men were stationed here. The Royal Naval Air Service flew the airships to relay details of U-boat sailings to naval surface vessels at their Holyhead base, which included motor launches, armed yachts, trawlers, and later, United States navy vessels. They patrolled from Bardsey to Dublin, the Isle of Man and Morecambe Bay and, when the convoy system was brought into action, escorted ships to safety.

The three years between 1915 and the end of the war were busy. By 1920 the airships had disappeared, and Mona was a ghost airfield. The Government Disposal Board sold the site to Anglesey County Council. It has since been used as an emergency airfield and for private flying, and recently a section close to the road has been developed as a business park.

A short distance after passing through Gwalchmai on the way to Holyhead, with the quarry to the right, the road crosses the little Afon Caradog and makes its way to Bryngwran. This is a ribbon village with little behind the main road. It looks across the Afon Crigyll valley towards Caergeiliog. The land to the west is marshy, low lying, the lake district of Anglesey. It is an area steeped in folklore and tradition, with a palpable atmosphere which exists in no other part of the island in spite of the proximity of the modern R.A.F. station at Valley.

A Welsh novelist who wrote early in the 20th century was born in Bryngwran, and it was the stories passed down to him about smuggling activity on the Crigyll estuary not far from his home that inspired him to write an adventure romance which has weathered the passage of time. *Madam Wen* has become one of the Welsh literary classics.

The author, William David Owen, attended the teacher-training college in Bangor before leaving his home in Bryngwran to take up his first teaching post at Clay Cross in Derbyshire. But he soon found that teaching was not for him, and he turned to journalism, no doubt with encouragement from his wife, Gwendoline, who was a writer. Eventually he studied law. Although called to the Bar he fell ill and could not continue his career. On doctor's orders he returned to Anglesey where, for a time, he supervised the Army Pensions Office in Llangefni, then opened his own solicitor's practice with offices in Llangefni and Rhosneigr.

Writing remained his main interest, so he took up his pen again. He co-operated in producing a brochure to tempt tourists to visit Rhosneigr. In it he told of the fascinating, mysterious hinterland and wrote of 'the famous Lady Robin Hood of North Wales, the notorious Madam Wen'. He had started to write a novel, *Dychweliad y Crwydryn* (The Return of the Wanderer) which appeared serialised in a Welsh newspaper. This dealt with life in an Anglesey village. When this ended, it was followed by weekly instalments of *Madam Wen, Arwres yr Ogof* (Madam Wen, Heroine of the Cave) which continued until 1914.

The story was published as a book in 1925, and second and third editions followed with the language updated. It is still available on public library shelves.

W.D. Owen's novel tells of Einir Wyn, a local beauty who had lost her inheritance through the Civil Wars. She led a gang of smugglers from her cave at Llyn Traffwll before she fell in love with the local squire. Llyn Traffwll can be approached at Llanfihangel yn Nhowyn, a short distance along a side road off the A5 between Bryngwran and Caergeiliog.

Valley

Valley, the village at the cross roads before the Stanley Embankment takes Telford's road on to Ynys Cybi *(Holy Island)*, is Anglesey's nearest approach to a New Town. Before Thomas Telford arrived in 1822 it barely existed.

The earlier route to Holyhead, if the traveller did not wish to risk crossing the sands at low tide, was by the stone causeway and bridge at Pont-Rhyd-Bont, known by non-Welsh speakers as Four Mile Bridge as it lies four miles from Holyhead.

There is evidence, however, of some early occupation in hut circles on the shores of the Inland Sea, and the name Beddmanarch on the strait dividing the islands suggests a monastic settlement in the area.

Valley lies within the parish of Llanynghenedl, whose church stood a short distance out of the village on the road to Cemaes. The churchyard is at the meeting of the A5025 with the old post road, B5109, from Bodedern. Now Valley has its own church of St Michael, an attractive building erected in 1881 and largely paid for by the Holyhead philanthropist and squire, William Owen Stanley of Penrhos. Some of the stones from the older parish church, now demolished, were used in an extension to St Michael's at Valley.

Telford's plan to carry his road across Beddmanarch

Bay on an embankment had the effect of shortening the journey by several miles, but its construction, like that at Malltraeth, was not without problems as in March 1824 part was destroyed by a storm.

The embankment is 1300 yards long, considerably wider at the base than at the top. When the railway to Holyhead was completed a station was built to the south west. The Stanley embankment was broadened to take the track and a tall dividing wall built – so that engines would not frighten horses on the road.

C.G. Harper in *The Holyhead Road*, written in 1902, refers to Valley as 'a modern village with a railway station'.

'A quarter of a mile beyond', he wrote, 'road and rail go side by side across the Stanley Sands, dividing Anglesey and Holy Island, the road on Telford's great mile-long embankment, and the rail on the left hid from sight by a dull masonry wall some sixteen or twenty feet high. The scene is still as melancholy as it was when Borrow tramped past with the broad channel a waste of sand at low tide and a furious salt water stream at the flood, rushing with great force through the arches in the middle of the embankment. The winds that boom and buzz across the flat shores and rank grasses and the waves lapping about the seaweed and rotting timbers of ancient wrecks give the place a sinister and mournful air'.

Some things do not change!

The name Valley came about as a result of the construction of the Stanley embankment. Workers had to dig a depression, a 'valley', to obtain rubble for the foundations. A small settlement developed nearby which eventually reached hamlet proportions, and it became, in common parlance, Valley. Latterly the Welsh translation, Dyffryn, has been used but that was not the original name.

As the railway emerged, the hamlet spread in that direction and the hamlet grew in to a village, with shops, chapels and public houses. Now Valley and Pont-Rhyd-Bont are almost connected.

The Inland Sea, the strip of water dividing Ynys Cybi from Anglesey at this point, is a nature lover's paradise. It has a unique tidal flow and its salt marsh is home to many species of plants.

In days gone by small boats were built on the shore of Beddmanarch Bay. They were wherries of around ten tons, resembling flat bottomed barges. There was also a breaker's yard. The cabin of one of the boats broken here was bought by the owner of the Valley Hotel to use on the shore as a summer house, but has since been destroyed.

Before the embankment was built, flooding was frequent over the low-lying fields at high water. Sluice doors improved the situation.

An early local historian tells of the building of the inner harbour at Holyhead in 1880, when a huge quantity of mud from the excavation was tipped on the field opposite the signal box at Valley, afterwards called 'Cae Mwd'.

Valley gained in importance with the opening of the workhouse by the Poor Law Guardians of the Holyhead Union in 1870. Records remain in the county archives, giving a picture of poverty which was a feature of country living in Victorian times and later. Eventually the building was converted into a hospital and this, in turn, was demolished when the new Stanley Hospital at Holyhead began to serve the population in the town and surrounding villages, and housing was built on the site.

In 1900 the Holyhead Board of Guardians gave permission to an elderly man to visit the workhouse to see the women with a view to marriage. None pleased him and he left, disappointed. But he changed his mind and returned the following day. The Welsh newspaper, *Y Clorianydd*, reported . . .

He informed the governors of one who was willing to marry, a widow with four children. He was asked if he would be willing to take all the family. He answered that one of the youngest would be sufficient. The Board agreed to this and freed the woman and child. The Board contributed thirty shillings to buy the woman clothes.

The A55 expressway has taken much of the traffic away from Valley but now the village is intersected by two national cycle routes, the N8 Holyhead to Cardiff, and the N5 Holyhead to Liverpool.

Bodedern

The importance of Bodedern to the community of hamlets in central Anglesey before Telford built his post road across the island began to wane as soon as traffic and travellers forsook the old road in favour of speed and greater comfort of the new.

Cottages were grouped around the old parish church of Saint Edeyrn, which is still the centre of the village. In days gone by this village centre bustled with activity. The inhabitants of Bodedern worked on the farms, on the nearby estates, or in one of the two wool-spinning mills with their dyehouses and fulling mill close by. There were eight fairs every year, one of them a hiring fair where farmers could hire labour for the following season. Petty sessions were held once a month. A National school was opened in 1822.

A press was set up in Bodedern during the 18th century, working, it is said, from a cottage known as Tŷ Cristion. It was founded by a peripatetic schoolmaster from Cardigan, John Rowlands, in the 1750s. John Rowlands had come to Bodedern as schoolmaster at one of the circulating schools of the period, and spent at least two seasons in the village. While here he printed poems, hymns, and religious books, but his efforts, say his critics, were not of a particularly high standard.

Early habitation of the area is evident through the existence of a burial mound and cromlech, at Treiorwerth and Presaddfed.

The Treiorwerth barrow was first excavated in 1870 and again almost a century later by archaeologists from the University of Wales at Bangor. Three lintel graves, one of a child, and possibly one or more dug graves were found.

The Rev. John Skinner, writing his reminiscences of *Ten Days Tour through Anglesey* in 1802, mentioned having visited the Presaddfed cromlech and marvelled at its size. He wrote 'Under this cromlech we were informed a whole family who had been ejected from their habitation sought shelter during the last winter'.

Bodedern parish church dates back many centuries. Saint Edeyrn is said to have been a seventh century Anglesey poet who was converted to Christianity and thereafter led a religious life. The nave of the church could be 14th century and was, in all probability, the old church building. This was extended in later years. Today visitors and communicants appreciate the memorials to local families and the carved communion rails and panelling.

The parish pump on the roadside, sheltered under a classical pediment, was presented by Lord Stanley of Alderley to the village in 1897, long before Bodedern had its piped water supply.

Three important families held sway in Bodedern at various stages in its history, in the houses of Presaddfed, Treiorwerth, and Mynydd-y-Gof. All three houses still exist.

The Bodedern area is famous for its early poets, who wrote their memorial verses to the early owners of

Presaddfed and Treiorwerth.

Hwfa ab Cynddelw was one of the wealthiest men among Anglesey's gentry during the reign of Edward III. His distinguished rank and the fact that he attended the king's coronation, bearing aloft the right side of the canopy over the monarchs head, gave him the right to hold the estate of Presaddfed in fee. He built the first house on the site.

When John Skinner visited Presaddfed in 1802, he was not impressed. 'An old mansion near the spot (the cromlech) was, we understand, the residence of Miss Buckley (sic), the lady who married King, Master of Ceremonies at Bath. The premises seem to be very much out of repair, having been untenanted for some time.'

Presaddfed lies close to Llyn Llywenan, off the road from Trefor leading into Bodedern, with Treiorwerth as its near neighbour. The burial chamber is on the lake shore, and the tumulus lies in the grounds of Treiorwerth.

Part of the present house of Presaddfed dates from 1686, but it was reconstructed considerably in 1821, after John Skinner had visited, and found the 1686 house so dilapidated. Writing in 1912, Filson Young recorded his impressions of Presaddfed in a privately published booklet. *A house in Anglesey,* in which he commented 'This house, although it has a personality of its own, is friendly and accommodating to those it shelters'.

Sir John Bulkeley, a member of an offshoot of the powerful Bulkeley family of Baron Hill, Beaumaris, lived at Presaddfed with his sister Margaret. To the consternation of the family Margaret married an Englishman of no particular social standing, in their opinion. He was James King, Master of Ceremonies at

Bath at a time when the rich and those aspiring to the height of fashion would spend the season there. James King was a well-known figure. Jane Austen mentions him in her novel, *Northanger Abbey*, and an engraving, showing a handsome man, can be seen in one of Bath's public buildings today. One would hardly expect to find a connection with Jane Austen in a small Anglesey village.

James King was born in Dublin. He held his position in Bath between 1785 and 1816, and a similar position in Cheltenham as the social seasons of the two spas did not coincide.

James had an illegitimate son, who was to be of great comfort to Margaret when she returned to Presaddfed after her husband's death. He spent the rest of his days in Anglesey.

Margaret's brother, Sir John, also married. He died before his wife, who later married again, this time the Rev. John Elias, the famous Welsh Nonconformist preacher. It was his second marriage, also.

James King's son's wife died in 1873 and he continued to live at Presaddfed with a housekeeper. A wandering tramp broke in to Presaddfed one night and attacked King in a small room on the ground floor, also attacking the housekeeper who had come to King's rescue. Local legend has it that King was murdered.

Relations between the Presaddfed family and Archdeacon Wynne Jones of Treiorwerth were not always harmonious. Archdeacon Jones was the vicar of Bodedern. Early in the 1830s the church was rebuilt and the vicar had been allotting pews. King was given four pews for himself and his tenants, but demanded that the allocation be reviewed as the Mynydd-y-Gof family had been given pews although they were Methodists. The vicar replied that any change would upset the arrangements of the choir, and deprecated 'any further disturbance of the singers to whose gratuitous services we are so much indebted at Bodedern'.

A descendent of Archdeacon Wynne Jones, the Rev. Hugh Wynne Jones (1751-1809) is said to have rebuilt Treiorwerth as it now stands, an elegant home on a rise which can be glimpsed through the trees from the road. Plans show Treiorwerth as it was in 1841, and again in 1886 after an addition had been made. This extension was demolished in 1979 and the present house is very similar to how it appeared when Hugh Wynne Jones rebuilt it.

The story of the disagreement between the owners of Presaddfed and Treiorwerth brings us to the family of Mynydd-y-Gof. David Roberts of Mynydd-y-Gof was a doctor and farmer, and a staunch Methodist. He and his wife Sarah married in 1815, and had ten children, three becoming famous in different spheres.

John Foulkes Roberts and his brother Hugh founded a hugely successful wholesale drapery business in Manchester – J.F. & H. Roberts. Robert, another son, wrote the story of the family for private circulation, which describes in detail the extent to which John became involved in the Welsh life of Manchester. He was Lord Mayor of the city in 1896/7. William, the eighth son, studied medicine, and after considerable experience in London, Paris and Berlin, was chief consultant at the Manchester Infirmary and taught medicine at Owens College, later Manchester University. He was knighted for his services to medicine.

Although not as brilliant as his brothers, Robert's

contribution to local history of the Bodedern area, through the story of his family, is vitally important. From it we can understand the situation of servants in an Anglesey country house, of the emphasis placed on religion, on education, and on current attitudes towards family life during the latter years of the 19th century. His reminiscences of life in Manchester, particularly in the cotton trade and in Manchester Welsh society, are equally important.

Llanddeusant, Llanfachraeth and Llanfechell

Central and north west Anglesey is an area of rolling fields. The lanes are quiet, even in the height of the tourist season. Call at the visitor centre at Llyn Alaw to learn about nature on the shores of this man-made lake, and you could well be alone, savouring the true atmosphere of the anglesey countryside.

Llyn Alaw, covering 777 acres, is a mile wide and three miles long. It holds 1640 million gallons of water. Filling began in November 1965 and the reservoir was full by January 1966. The official opening took place on the day of the Aberfan disaster in South Wales.

This is an area of small villages, unprepossessing at first glance yet with interesting associations. They are communities which have produced highly individual characters, some of whom have left their mark across the world, others having left us a penetrating insight into Anglesey of the past.

The sails of the restored windmill at Llanddeusant stand above the village, reminding the visitor that Anglesey was the home of over sixty mills as far back as the 14th century although, in those days, most were powered by water. But Anglesey's climate is dry. There are no fast-flowing rivers, and in dry summers some of them decrease to a mere trickle. This proved a problem in the days when the fertile soil of the island grew large amounts of grain which had to be milled. The population of Anglesey increased during the 14th century so there was greater demand. The main weather feature of the island has always been the wind, so this was harnessed, and windmills began to appear on the landscape.

Travelling around Anglesey today one sees many derelict windmills. One of the last to grind was Melin Llynon at Llanddeusant which, now restored, is an unusual sight in an island where once so many operated.

So what brought about the demise of the windmills in Anglesey?

During the latter years of the 19th century cheap grain from America began to be imported into Britain. The agricultural emphasis in Anglesey changed to cattle rearing. The industrial revolution saw the invention of new machinery and techniques. It was no longer financially viable to attempt to sell locally milled grain to the extent which had been done in the past, as cheap transport made buying cheaper flour produced from English steam-powered mills more attractive. Millers found it difficult to obtain labour, as it was apparent that the industry was in decline. Repairs following storms were costly. The mills which still operated were continued as part of a general farming operation, not as a business on their own.

Melin Llynon in Llanddeusant struggled on until the 1930s when it fell into disrepair. Acute storm damage in the 1950s blew off the cap and damaged most of the sails. In 1978 the farm and the mill were sold to Anglesey Borough Council who made the highly popular promise to restore the mill 'for future generations of islanders to enjoy and learn about their heritage' – a decision which has proved wise as Melin Llynon is now one of Anglesey's top tourist attractions.

Restoration revealed many problems. The first phase during the three years 1981-3 involved clearing the tower of fallen masonry and rusted machinery, salvaging what could be used again and replacing timbers. Lincolnshire millwrights were commissioned to do the restoration, and much of the preparatory work was done in their workshops. The sails were made there. The day they arrived by road at Llynon gave an excuse for celebration!

The cost of restoring Llynon was £120,000, finance being made available through Anglesey Borough Council, the Shell Oil Revenue Fund and the Historic Buildings Council for Wales. The mill was re-opened by the Marquess of Anglesey on May 11, 1984. When the wind blows in the right direction and at the appropriate strength, the sails turn once again and grain is ground for sale to visitors.

Melin Llynon is what is termed 'a tower mill', where the top cap can be turned for the sails to catch the wind.

A short distance away stands Melin Hywel, on the bank of the river Alaw. This is a watermill whose history goes back several centuries. According to documents, there was a mill on the site in the 14th century. Watermills in those days were usually the property of the Welsh princes, but this was privately owned and named after the owner, Hywel ap Rhys. In later years ownership passed from generation to generation of the Williams family. The problems caused by the flow of water decreasing during dry summers was recognised in early days, when the owner built a dam upstream, the flow being controlled by a floodgate.

As was then the custom, the miller was paid in kind, receiving a percentage of what was ground as a toll.

Melin Hywel continued to operate until it was repaired and restored in 1975. Norman Squire Johnson, the architect responsible for the work, was awarded a prize in a national architectural preservation competition. There is a plaque to that effect commemorating the success of the conservation on the wall of the mill.

Grinding stones for Anglesey mills came from a variety of sources, locally, from France and Scandinavia. One pair of stones at Melin Hywel came from the Rhine valley.

The importance of the two mills at Llanddeusant overshadows the story of the village itself. The parish church has the unusual dedication to two saints, hence the name Llanddeusant, 'the church of the two saints'. These were Marcellinus and Marcellus, one succeeding the other as Pope during the fourth century. The church was completely rebuilt in 1868, but the font and memorials are from the previous building.

During the 18th century the parish suffered from the practice, common at the time, of being in the care of an un-educated curate while a vicar or rector, who had several parishes to oversee, lived elsewhere and rarely visited. The curate at Llanddeusant at the time was said to have been 'but a common labourer, nothing even of a School scholar', and who could manage only 'an unintelligible jargon of a sermon'.

Llanfachraeth is a string of dwellings either side of the road from Valley to Cemaes and Amlwch. The village has a chapel at Pont yr Arw which bears a slate plaque on its front elevation in memory of Thomas Jesse Jones who died in 1950, 'teacher and philanthropist'. His philanthropy benefited people world wide.

Thomas Jesse Jones was born in Llanfachraeth in 1875. He was brought up at *Y Bedol Aur*, the local inn which, in those days, was a community centre for the village as well as a place to stay for visitors, preachers, educators and government officers. This is where farmers would meet and air their problems and an atmosphere of lively debate was created which young Thomas absorbed quietly.

When he was nine years old, the family emigrated to America to join Thomas's uncle who was in business in Ohio. Thomas and his brother received a sound education. In 1891 he was at university and by 1904 had graduated M.A., B.D., and Ph.D.

Great social changes were taking place in America, avidly appreciated by Thomas Jesse Jones, and he began to undertake work to integrate black and white communities. These were formative years for him, to be followed by wide experience in sociological fields. He joined the federal government in Washington as chief statistician where he was regarded as having expert knowledge.

A long period followed, working for a Foundation concerned with the erection of tenement dwellings in New York City for poor families, and for overseeing educational facilities for negroes, American Indians and needy white students.

During the first world war he served in France as a welfare officer with special responsibility for negro students.

Thomas Jesse Jones's Baptist beginnings at Pont yr Arw

led to his support of that denomination throughout his life. He was appointed to lead commissions relating to social conditions among ethnic minorities, world-wide. All this was a far cry from his home at *Y Bedol Aur*, and his Sunday chapel attendance at Llanfachraeth, but he did not forget his roots and presented a bible to the chapel in memory of his mother and father in 1933. Anglesey remembers him with the plaque to his memory.

A few miles along the road to Cemaes Llanfaethlu stands on a rise looking south towards the sails of Melin Llynon.

The Beer Act of 1830 had extended drinking opportunities throughout Wales. Ale houses were crowded, even Sunday church attendance was followed by heavy drinking by parishioners and clergy alike, until the new freedom became a serious social problem. This was counteracted eventually in several ways – by the introduction of temperance and total abstinence societies, which were popular in Anglesey, and the opening of coffee houses. Lady Reade, a local lady who owned two taverns in Llanfaethlu, closed them and provided a coffee house where villagers and visitors could meet. The building stands today, a testimony to her concern for the welfare of the common people.

Llanfechell, in the hinterland between Cemaes and Llyn Alaw, is especially important to those interested in the history of Anglesey because it was the home of the prolific 18th century diarist, William Bulkeley, who spent his life at Brynddu near the village church.

William Bulkeley has bequeathed to successive generations a vivid picture of life in the Anglesey countryside of his day.

Reading his diary, one is left with an impression of a man who did not suffer fools gladly, who was deeply involved in his church, in local politics and social administration, a lover of his garden and a family man whose children caused him much heartache following the early death of his wife. He wrote often with wry humour which brings him to life through the words on the page. No portrait of him exists, but his written words are enough for readers over two centuries later to form their own image of him.

William Bulkeley was a landowner, so farming was part of his life.

The parish church of St Mechell stands in the village centre. The nave and part of the chancel are from the 12th century. Several alterations and additions to the fabric have been made over the years. Llanfechell church has a capped tower, one of very few in Anglesey to have this feature.

At the time when William Bulkeley wrote his diary, several other churches in nearby villages were experiencing the incompetence of curates, but Llanfechell had its resident rector, so the village was well cared for spiritually. The church held sway over the social life of its parishioners. Patronal festivals were celebrated – with games and stalls in the churchyard and a vast amount of drinking. Bulkeley describes the goings-on with the facility of a modern-day journalist. He made no bones about the fact that the rector irritated him on occasions and, like worshippers everywhere in those days, he had to endure long sermons.

'The Parson finished ye sermon that he began on the 19th instant. We were kept so long in church by reason of the Sermon, Sacrament and reading of the Act of Parliament against prophane (sic) cursing and swearing that it was above half an hour past one when we went out, the sun shining upon the eastern pannel (sic) of my seat.' December 26, 1736. All this on a cold Sunday with no heating in church!

On Easter Eve, April 1, 1738, he recorded 'the parson spent above two hours in expounding or rather confounding ye Catechism, which being originally misterious (sic) if not in many places absurd. I think he made it ten times worse'.

The charity school at Llanfechell was where the prowess of young William Jones, son of a local farmer, was discovered in the late 17th century. His ability with figures, at an early age, was astounding. His future was sponsored by Lord Bulkeley of Beaumaris, on whose land the family worked, and William was apprenticed to a London merchant on leaving school. He was able to travel abroad and obtained a teaching post on a man-o'-war in the West Indies, where his methods were so successful that he was recommended as a tutor to several gentry families back home in England. While doing this tutorial work he continued to research mathematics, wrote several books, and was elected a Fellow of the Royal Society.

The quiet villages of Anglesey have produced some notable characters.

Llanfairynghornwy

Some of the smallest, most remote villages in Anglesey have been home to people who have created ripples nationwide in industry, commerce, education, politics, medicine and the world of letters. As case in point is the tiny village of Llanfairynghornwy, tucked away from main roads in the north west corner of the island. Its parish boundaries reach down to the sea and, indeed, across the sea to The Skerries.

The farms and houses are scattered, linked by narrow lanes. The medieval church of St Mary was much restored during the busy period of church restoration in the reign of Queen Victoria, and was once one of the most lucrative livings on the island.

But before this, in 1821, the Rev. James Williams, curate at Llanfairpwllgwyngyll and Penmynydd, followed his father as rector at Llanfairynghornwy when John Williams retired, and three years later had built a fine rectory nearby which was to be his home until he died in 1872.

John Williams, father of James, had held the office of chaplain at Windsor. He petitioned King George IV on behalf of his son when the king visited Holyhead on his return from Ireland. The king granted his request and instructed the Bishop of Bangor that James was to succeed his father in Llanfairynghornwy when the living became vacant.

During the 19th century, a period when there was a flurry of church restoration on the island, some rectors and vicars were also amateur architects. Where parishes had little money to spend to commission a professional architect, their efforts, for the most part, were the means of saving ancient buildings from ruin.

James Williams was one who had a flair for 'design and build' as it would be termed today. It is thanks to his efforts that the little church of St Mary was improved so tastefully.

At the time James was appointed to the parish, pluracy of livings was widely operated, with clergy officiating in more than one parish and appointing their own curates to act on their behalf while they reaped income from tithes and some did little pastoral work themselves. But James Williams was more conscientious and was determined to look after his own flock.

Born in Treffos, Llansadwrn, in 1790, he was well educated, becoming a Fellow of Jesus College, Oxford, and Canon and Chancellor of Bangor Cathedral. As well as running a parish, he was a magistrate and had a long-standing interest in agriculture.

James Williams married Frances Lloyd, who was related by marriage to Samuel Butler and a friend of the Darwin family. The weather was stormy when the couple arrived at their new parish. James took his bride down to the coast for Frances to see the awesome sight of a storm at sea. What they saw, to their horror, was a sailing ship, the *Alert*, helpless on the rocks. She sank almost immediately. One hundred and forty lives were lost. This tragedy made such an impression on the young couple that they vowed to work to provide the means of saving life around the treacherous coast of Anglesey in future storms.

James had useful family connections and his social standing was such that he could turn his powers of persuasion to good use. The money began to arrive, enough to provide a boat to be used solely for life-saving. This was berthed at Cemlyn, James being the first coxswain. The next development was the formation of The Anglesey Association for the Preservation of Life from Shipwreck, in 1828.

Frances, like many ladies of her time, painted in watercolours, so to support her husband in his fund-raising she had lithographs made of a painting she had done when George IV landed at Holyhead from Ireland, which she sold for seven shillings each, the money being given to the Association.

During 1833 over fifty ships were lost off the shores of Anglesey. The need for lifeboats around the island was desperate.

As well as his parish duties, James Williams helped to design the boats and the rocket launching equipment used. Between 1829 and 1856, when the Anglesey Association became part of the Royal National Lifeboat Institution, over 400 lives were saved by Anglesey lifeboats.

James's bravery at sea was acknowledged in 1835 when the R.N.L.I. awarded him its Gold Medal for rescuing the crews of two ships. One was the *Active* of Belfast, grounded as she neared Cemaes in a storm. It was impossible to launch a boat, but James Williams rode his horse into the sea, threw a grapnel into the ship's shrouds which made it possible for the lifeboat to be hauled out to the *Active* to take off the crew of five. Again, a year later, he showed bravery by superintending the difficult rescue of fourteen men, the crew of the *Sarah* which had been driven on to the rocks at Trecastell. The ship sank a few minutes after the men were saved.

There were many more stories of the bravery of this intrepid clergyman. Frances Williams was equally brave. She sailed with her husband in the Cemlyn boat to the Skerries where the lighthouse keeper was ill, attended to him, then returned, making both passages in rough weather.

James and Frances Williams never shirked their parochial duties. In their handsome new rectory they entertained, painted, enjoyed harp music, studied geology and agriculture, and encouraged education locally. Theirs was a full, active life.

James and Frances had four children. The oldest son, Owen Lloyd Williams, continued his parents' dedication to saving life at sea by becoming, in his turn, coxswain of the Cemlyn lifeboat. He, too, entered the church. While rector of Boduan on the Llŷn peninsula he took charge of the Porthdinllaen and Abersoch boats and received R.N.L.I. awards.

James and Frances Williams lie buried in the churchyard at Llanfairynghornwy.

The Skerries and Harry Furlong's Rocks off shore saw many shipwrecks over the years, but none more famous than that of the *Mary*, the first royal yacht.

Mary had been presented to Charles, Pretender to the English throne, by William, Prince of Orange, but she was found unsuited to sailing conditions on the River Thames so had been put into service to carry important passengers between England and Ireland.

During March 1675 *Mary* was wrecked close to The Skerries, where she sank. She remained forgotten until, in 1971, sub aqua club members on a dive chanced to come across two of her bronze guns. This encouraged a more exhaustive search. Now 1500 artefacts from the wreck are in the care of the Maritime Museum at Liverpool.

The Ordnance Survey map marks The Skerries as 'Ynysoedd y Moelrhoniaid *(Islands of the seals)* Llanfairynghornwy det'. When Frances Williams attended her lighthouse keeper parishioner the light on The Skerries had been improved, as a new lighthouse had been built in 1804/5. The Skerries rocks lie on the shipping lane between Liverpool and Ireland. They had long been a major hazard to shipping until, in 1714, the leaseholder, William Trench, was given permission to erect a light. He paid the Crown a rent of £5 a year, for which he had the right to levy dues of one penny per ship and twopence per ton of cargo. The light was coal-fired, laid in a basket.

Dues were easy to evade, however, or William Trench was not as careful as he should have been about collecting them. When he died in 1729 he was financially ruined. His daughter inherited The Skerries and an Act of Parliament was passed giving her sole rights. By 1834 new owners had taken over, and they refused an offer by Trinity House to buy as by then it had become a profitable investment. But in 1841 Trinity House finally bought the islands and the light, for the princely sum of £44,984. It was the last privately owned lighthouse to pass into their ownership.

Trench's light, a round tower with an open bucket-shaped basket, consumed 80-100 tons of coal a year. The 1804/5 lighthouse had an oil light with reflectors. This remained in use until 1927 when it was changed to electricity. In 1987 it was converted to automation and there is no longer a lighthouse keeper as the light is controlled by Trinity House from the operations control at Harwich.

Today's light has a range of 29 miles. It flashes twice every ten seconds and a fog signal sounds twice every minute. Servicing the light at The Skerries, as on most other lighthouses today, is carried out by Trinity House inspectors using helicopters for access. The Skerries has a pad on the rocks.

Mynachdy, a farmhouse on the edge of the Llanfairynghornwy parish between the village and Hen Borth is a Tudor period house which has, it is claimed, an underground passageway leading to the shore, no doubt a useful hide-away for smugglers and their loot. Smuggling was rife here during the late 18th century.

A local smuggler, Dannie Lukie, was out one night in stormy weather when he found a ship in distress. The crew of three had taken to a small boat and were battling against heavy seas to row to the shore.

He managed to reach them, and found a man and two terrified boys aboard. The man had died, but Lukie took the boys ashore close to Mynachdy which was then the home of Dr Lloyd, who cared for them until they recovered. Neither boy could speak English nor Welsh, but Dr Lloyd believed them to be Spanish. It is not known what happened to one, but the other, who was given the name Evan Thomas, remained at Mynachdy where he worked on the farm. He showed great interest in Dr Lloyd's practice. The doctor allowed Evan to accompany him on his rounds, having noticed his ability to mend broken bones after he had successfully set a chicken's leg on the farm.

As Evan grew older, this ability increased. Whenever there was a need for bone-setting, Evan went along and, at the same time, learnt about surgery from his mentor.

Evan Thomas married, and the couple had four sons. The third son, Richard, inherited his father's gift. He had been christened Richard ap Evan Thomas, but later abbreviated his name to Richard Evans. Other members of the family and their descendants were also bone-setters, practising on Anglesey, in Liverpool and elsewhere.

One became especially famous – Sir Robert Jones, whose work in orthopaedics saw the transformation of the Agnes Hunt Convalescent Homes at Gobowen into an orthopaedic centre of great renown. The family is also accredited with the development of the 'Thomas splint' and the 'Thomas caliper' which were to prove of such great value during the treatment of first world war casualties, and have been in use ever since.

Cemaes

With the current demand for 'getting away from it all', it is not surprising that so many looking for a break from everyday stress in the cities should choose Cemaes. Nestling to one side of a beautiful natural bay, this northern-most village in Anglesey appears, given the weather, to offer everything one could wish for in the way of complete relaxation.

Yet it has not always been so. Until the railways made the transport of goods so much easier, Anglesey's little ports were busy with both import and export trade. Cemaes was no exception. But more of this later.

Although Cemaes has its newer church, built in 1865, the village is in the parish of Llanbadrig, whose ancient church stands apart, exposed on a cliff top on the eastern side of the bay. This, so legend has it, was where Saint Patrick first set foot on Britain, and is one of the oldest ecclesiastical sites in the country. The saint is said to have established a cell here. There may be other churches elsewhere dedicated to Saint Patrick, but this is the only one with a personal connection. The saint was shipwrecked off shore, so the the story goes, and founding the cell was his way of showing gratitude for safe deliverance. This took place around A.D. 440, and ever since that time people have worshipped at Llanbadrig church.

The present building dates from the 14th century. There is a palpable air of antiquity here, although several changes have taken place since then, but these have done little to disperse the atmosphere which permeates this ancient building.

The Victorians changed the face of many of our old churches, not always for the better. In 1884 the local squire, Lord Stanley of Alderley, restored Llanbadrig. He provided £700 towards the cost, with the stipulation that the new church decor should include elements of the Moslem faith, to which he ascribed, hence the preponderance of red, white and blue in the stained glass and the blue tiles around the sanctuary.

A mosaic panel shows the Good Shepherd carrying a lamb – although showing a Moslem design influence this is unusual as the Moslem faith does not allow for depicting a human figure or an animal. An earlier decoration is the Ichthus stone, found in the wall of the church as it was being restored, which shows a fish and a palm tree.

Latterly, restorations of Llanbadrig church have been fraught with problems. In 1985 parishioners were forced into a programme of conservation and restoration when vandals set fire to the church. A stupendous money-raising effort for a small community, supported by parishioners and visitors, paid for a £15,000 restoration. On the eve of the re-consecration fire destroyed the work once again, which entailed yet another appeal and another period of work, this time costing double the first amount.

The graveyard at Llanbadrig is open to the weather, and there are stories of burials having to be delayed because gales made it impossible for them to be carried out to time.

But back to the village itself.

When local small industries were busy, Cemaes saw many ships arriving and leaving the bay. Local people fished for a living, and the village became famous for its salted herring. Coal was imported, as were wines from France. Limestone, corn, bricks, lime and ochre were exported. There was thriving ship building industry, as during the 19th century ships from one hundred to four hundred tons were built here. The Klondyke brickworks, to the far side of the present by-pass from the village, produced bricks which were carried down to the harbour by a narrow gauge railway, to be loaded on to ships. The line is now a pleasant footpath alongside the river Wygyr.

Centuries ago the hamlet was known as Castell Iorwerth, after the Welsh Prince Iorwerth who held court on this northern coast. The later name, Cemais, refers to the bends in the river Wygyr which flows into the sea here. The anglicised form, Cemaes Bay, could have come about with the influx of English holidaymakers when the village became a resort with the opening of the railway across Anglesey to Amlwch, and to distinguish it from Cemais in Montgomeryshire.

Local fishermen built a small stone pier for their own convenience for landing catches, but this was washed away in a severe storm in 1828. Ishmael Jones, a local sea captain and entrepreneur, spear-headed a movement towards building a new pier. But financial promises were slow to be fulfilled. Liverpool businessman, full of enthusiasm for Ishmael's plan at the outset, cooled when asked to produce financial proof of their support. Local farmers and businesses met lean times and so they, too, were unable to honour their promises. So Ishmael Jones financed the new pier himself. It was completed in 1835.

Another problem regarding the harbour arose during the 1840s when W. Bulkeley Hughes, who owned land on the edge of the bay, spent a considerable sum on improving the harbour. His tenant was prosecuted for 'infringing the rights of the Crown in respect of the foreshore', but Bulkeley Hughes, in his defence, argued that 'rights of wreck and shore' had been granted to his ancestor in 1609 by the then king, and these rights still held good. The case was heard at Chester Crown court and aroused much interest, especially when Bulkeley Hughes's appeal was upheld. There was great rejoicing locally, with flags flying and bonfires lit to celebrate the outcome.

Over the years more improvements were made until, in 1889, another great storm did more damage. That pier was then repaired and extended in 1900. The local newspaper, *Y Clorianydd*, reported the conclusion of the work . . .

(in translation)
The Pier Supper: A week last Tuesday a group gathered at the village hall to enjoy a celebratory supper on the occasion of the completion of the pier. Mr Samuel Thomas, the contractor for the re-building, provided the meal. The village is unanimous in praise of Mr Thomas who has completed this work, as he does everything he undertakes, excellently and successfully. The new pier, as it is called, will be a decided asset to the village, and it has also improved the appearance of the beach. Twenty-eight workers attended, all very complimentary of Mr Thomas, and also the vicar. After the meal congratulatory speeches were given followed by one or two songs, and two very pleasant hours were

spent. The hope is that the pier, as it now appears, will successfully withstand every storm for generations to come.

Nowadays, as the old industries in the area have virtually disappeared and tourism has taken over, fishing boats and pleasure vessels are the main users. The new industries of nuclear and wind power need no pier nor harbour at Cemaes Bay.

With the introduction of nuclear energy, the headland of Wylfa was chosen as a suitable site for a power station, and construction of the Wylfa Magnox Power Station began in 1963. Reactor 1 started generating in January 1971, and reactor 2 followed in June of that year. Magnox Electric PLC merged with British Nuclear Fuels Ltd. in 1998.

On a typical day Wylfa will supply 23mKWH of electricity enough to meet the needs of two cities the size of Liverpool. The gaunt buildings of the station on the Cemaes Bay skyline serve to remind holidaymakers that industry is never far away, even from this charming bay. On the other side, in the Amlwch direction, the windmills of the Rhydygroes windfarm give a similar reminder. These twenty-four wind turbines, set up in 1992, contribute a considerable amount of electricity to the national grid annually, as they operate when the wind speed in this gusty part of the island is between five and twenty-five metres a second.

The hub of the village of Cemaes Bay is its High Street, which is dominated by the Village Hall.

David Hughes, a 19th century Cemaes carpenter, left to work in the rapidly expanding house-building trade in Liverpool, where eventually he set up on his own as a builder, and became wealthy. He always regarded Cemaes as his home, and built a house, *Wylfa* on the promontory on which the Magnox Power Station now stands. In a generous gesture to the community he built the Village Hall at a cost of £2,500, which was opened with ceremony in July 1898.

The Hall has a fifty-feet high tower with three clock faces, which dominates the High Street.

The accommodation included a large hall for public meetings, a reading room and a restaurant. Over a century later, David Hughes's magnanimous gift is still appreciated by many local people who use it for their social gatherings.

Cemaes has seen many changes which have come about through developments nationally, like the emergence of a railway system which, although the track never reached Cemaes, accounted for the transport of goods from Cemaes and Amlwch to be diverted from the sea to the fast overland mode of transport. Tourism saved Cemaes, and it continues to be one of the area's main industries.

Recently Cemaes residents, intent on improving matters commercial, have set up Cymry Cemaes. At its base in the High Street, the centre offers tuition in new technology to anyone of any age. The move has proved widely popular. In the same building, opposite the Village Hall, is a Heritage Centre and a cafe which welcomes tourists, campers, walkers. A branch of that company arranges the very popular Celtic Festival held in the village during the summer. The foot and mouth epidemic disrupted events during 2001, but it is hoped the Festival will be established as a yearly occurrence in the future.

Initially Cymry Cemaes was helped by the Anglesey advisory organisation to encourage local business, Menter Môn, but latterly more aid has come from local businesses. One imagines David Hughes, the Cemaes Local-boy-made-good, would be in favour.

Llannerchymedd

Visitors to Llannerchymedd, unaware of its past, can have little appreciation of the village's importance to the agricultural community in days gone by, before Llangefni grew in stature to overtake it. Markets and fairs drew the crowds from the outlying farms and hamlets to converge on the bustling traders whose stalls lined its wide street below the church.

Samuel Lewis, in his *Topography of Wales* (1833), said Llannerchymedd appeared 'to have derived its progressive increase in extent and importance from its central situation. Previously to the commencement of the parliamentary war it had become a very populous village and as such set forth a petition . . . which was granted in 1657. This market, with the exception of that of Beaumaris, was the only one in the whole island and constituted a chief source of the prosperity . . . until the year 1785 when a market was granted to Llangevni' (sic).

He referred to the parish church of St Mary as 'a spacious structure with a lofty square tower at the west end. It is the joint property of the families of Llwydiarth and Bodelwyddan who have always kept it in a tolerable state of repair'.

In recent years the church has closed, as it faces a bill of thousands of pounds for urgent repairs.

The building has a medieval tower. The only other early feature is the doorway between the nave and the tower. The church bell is possibly from the 18th century. The font, a small octagonal gritstone bowl with a chamfered base, dates from the 14th century and some of the silver plate, two cups and a salver, is mid-18th century.

The church, apart from the tower, was altered in 1844 then re-built in 1850 at the time when there was much restoration and re-building of parish churches on the island, no fewer than twenty-seven being re-built and most of the remainder receiving some restorative attention inside or outside. Most of the work was entrusted to architect Henry Kennedy, who settled in Bangor. The churches he designed were simple, intended for parishes where there was little money to spend. They were not impressive, and had very little character.

The name Llannerchymedd refers to a glade where mead was distilled. It is thought likely that one of the earliest distilleries in Wales was to be found here.

Fairs in Anglesey towns and villages were necessary both to the economy and the standard of living. They were also eagerly anticipated social occasions by a populace which rarely travelled beyond a few miles from home.

Fairs were held four or five times a year on fixed dates. Llannerchymedd held five, and also a Wednesday market. Merchants came from as far afield as Lancashire and Yorkshire. They offered a greater variety of merchandise than could be found in the local shops. Here one could buy cattle, horses, foodstuffs, clothes, cloth, leather and durable household goods. The Llannerchymedd fairs were reputed to be the best showground for stallions. For the more affluent customer they provided an opportunity to stock up with essentials. The poor enjoyed the fairs as a chance to look, to admire, to wish for the wherewithal to buy, and to enjoy the spectacle. The fairs also gave local tradesmen the chance to fill their shelves.

The fairs were musical events, too. The fiddle, the harp and ballad singing could be heard mingling with the cries of the vendors. Wandering minstrels and ballad singers played and sang for their living, and were always sure of a welcome even though, in the early 19th century, Llannerchymedd was a nonconformist stronghold where the Methodists could be expected to frown on such 'decadent' entertainment. There was even dancing in the streets. It is said that one ballad singer who made a regular appearance was a man from Caernarfon, dressed in a tailcoat and sporting a chestfull of medals.

As it became easier and cheaper to buy manufactured goods, the shops began to stock more variety and the fairs lost their purpose.

In 1831 the first Anglesey Wool Fair was held. These wool fairs were held alternately at Llangefni and Llannerchymedd. They had a specific purpose and were patronised by farmers who, as well as buying and selling, could be taught how to dip and shear sheep if they had a mind to learn new methods.

Farmers in the area of Llannerchymedd knew about diversification well before the term was given its present connotation. Many carried on domestic weaving as a side-line, an industry which persisted in Anglesey long after factories were established. The weavers supplied local needs, spinning yarn from the wool of their own sheep.

The cobblers of Llannerchymedd were well known during the 19th century. In 1833 it was estimated that over

250 worked in the trade, which experienced an upsurge when the copper mines at Parys Mountain developed. They also made footwear for the Caernarfonshire quarry workers. The industry flourished in Llannerchymedd until the 1860s but declined rapidly in the following years as boots and shoes from Northamptonshire, factory-made, began to appear in the fairs and shops, to be sold far cheaper and, where women's shoes were concerned, in more fashionable styles.

Llannerchymedd clogs consisted of leather uppers tacked to soles of alder, made in boot or shoe styles. Iron rims were fixed to the lower edges of the sole which raised the clog above the ground, so protecting it from wear.

There is a record of a strike by wage-earning cobblers in Llannerchymedd in 1865, when they met in The Kings Head to formulate a demand for a rise of a groat (fourpence) for making a pair of shoes. The employers offered twopence, which was accepted.

The 19th century saw the disappearance of many of the old handicrafts because of mechanisation and the opening of factories.

Changes in manufacturing brought problems to the country workers. In 1880 the local parliamentary candidate, also a local squire and landowner, provided work for sixty cobblers who were suffering financially because of the public's growing preference for factory-made shoes. By the end of the century the number of cobblers in Llannerchymedd had dwindled to a handful and they were employed mainly in mending shoes produced in the English factories. The demise of the Parys Mountain copper industry also contributed to the situation.

Llannerchymedd was, at one time, famous for its snuff. Called 'Llwch mân Llannerchymedd' (Llannerchymedd Fine Dust) it was popular around the 1840s, but as taking snuff went out of fashion the industry declined and eventually disappeared.

Samuel Lewis in 1833 wrote 'The manufacture of high-dried Welsh snuff, closely resembling in its quality the celebrated Irish snuff, namely Lundy Foote's, for which this partly became a substitute, has been established here upon an extensive scale'.

But he went on to criticise the business acumen of the local snuff manufacturers and said the industry could have been even more productive had it been run more efficiently.

Another, more 'tasteful' small industry carried out in the village was the production of 'India Rock' which was so popular to the sweet-toothed buyers at all the Anglesey fairs.

The village became known for its cultural activity, being dubbed 'The Athens of Anglesey'. Many poets, musicians and performers have been associated with Llannerchymedd over the years.

During the 19th century Llannerchymedd was known as a centre for printing. This was instigated by an Independant minister, William Williams, when, in 1831, he began to publish a monthly magazine called *Y Sylwedydd* (The Observer). This was printed by Enoch Jones. It was intended for readers in an agricultural community but also included news from over the border and even overseas. Local activities were reported, and there was some poetry. Enoch Jones's press was responsible for producing pamphlets and leaflets, and he published at least five books, mostly on religious topics.

A Welsh writer, O. Gaianydd Williams, describes Llannerchymedd of the 19th century as a quiet, kindly place. The villagers were Welsh, no English visitors came to spend the summer there as they did in Beaumaris. There was a family atmosphere, where everyone knew everyone else.

The community spirit in Anglesey villages before the outside world became so easily accessible was tangible. During the Boer War, the victory at Ladysmith was celebrated enthusiastically in Llannerchymedd, as a newspaper report of 1900 describes . . .

On Friday afternoon Mr Joseph Crewdson, Llangefni, conveyed the Llangefni Band at his own expense to Llannerchymedd to join in the celebrations following the splendid victory at Ladysmith. To his surprise, all the schoolchildren awaited the visitors, carrying banners and wearing suitable colours. As soon as the band and patriots from Llangefni arrived, a procession formed, led by Mr Griffiths of the Board School and Mr John Owen, the Kings Head Hotel, and proceeded along the main street until they reached the residence of Dr W. Evans, where the band played. They returned to the Square, where they played 'Rule, Britannia' and 'God Save the Queen' to enthusiastic acclaim, Mr William Thomas, the bandmaster, leading with his customary skill. It was all a strong demonstration of the loyalty of the people of Llannerchymedd and their joy at the British victory.

Penysarn and Llaneilian

Penysarn (or Pensarn, in local parlance) is a small village now by-passed by the Menai Bridge-Amlwch road. Had one travelled this way before the copper industry developed at Parys Mountain, there would be little to be seen except a rough road from Dulas to Amlwch, with a causeway crossing marshy land near what is the middle of the present village. This was called Sarn yr Offeiriad Du (the causeway of the black priest). The first cottages were built on the higher, drier ground, and by 1839 the area was called Penysarn (the head of the causeway).

From the 1760s the Parys and Mona copper mines were developing to become the largest in the world. Housing was needed for the miners, so Penysarn came into being as a village. Ancillary industries developed, and these included clog-making for the miners.

Today the derelict building on the top of Parys Mountain overlooks Penysarn and the sleepy, now tidy village, remembers its past. Today's workers find employment elsewhere, in Amlwch, Llangefni and even as far away as Bangor.

The copper industry came into its own in the 18th century when the Admiralty ruled that the bottom of every warship should be covered with copper sheeting. The East India Company gave the same directive regarding its merchant ships. So landowners began to excavate their land for evidence of the existence of copper, for their own financial gain. In 1768 a rich vein was discovered on Parys Mountain, and so began a period of intensive mining which made some entrepreneurs very wealthy indeed.

By the end of the 18th century around 2,300 tons of copper were being mined here annually. Some 1,200 men and women and children were employed at this time, some of them had been agricultural workers who came into the industry tempted by higher rates of pay. The women, called 'Copper Ladies', broke up the ore into small pieces, working in sheds on the mountain. They wore a leather glove on the left hand and wielded a hammer in the right hand.

The Copper Ladies worked twelve hours each day, placing large pieces of ore on a knocking-stone and breaking it into small, more manageable pieces. They wore a uniform dress of homespun, an apron, and a yellow cloth tied around the head under a tall hat. They were regarded as distinctive characters.

The company manufactured its own coins, copper tokens now referred to as Parys Mountain pennies and halfpennies. It is sometimes possible to come across these today, in antique shops and car boot sales.

The industry developed so quickly that living accommodation for workers coming into the area with their families was roughly built. Most of these cottages were in Amlwch, where the population expanded rapidly, but this was also the type of housing which formed the village of Penysarn in its early days.

Every area has its characters, and the copper industry

at Parys Mountain was no exception. Cadi Rondol was a Copper Lady, and also a lady of easy virtue, said to be the best swearer in the district! The pathways through the workings, which she frequented, were known as 'llwybrau Cadi Rondol' (Cathy Rondol's paths). It was said she later reformed after being impressed by the famous Methodist preacher, John Elias.

In the village today are two plaques to men who were closely connected with Penysarn – Llew Llwyfo and Bedwyr Lewis Jones.

Lewis William Lewis (Llew Llwyfo) was one of the most gifted men of the 19th century. Born in Penysarn in 1831, he went to work with his father in the Parys Mountain copper mines when he was only eight years old. The family then moved to Bangor when the railway was being built, and Lewis was apprenticed to a Bangor grocer. He had been interested in music and literature from an early age, although his schooling had been fragmentary and brief. In Bangor he began to write for the press.

In 1850 Lewis returned to Anglesey to work in a Holyhead draper's shop and, after marrying a year later, moved back to Penysarn where he opened his own drapery business. But Lewis's mind was on literature, poetry and music, and he turned more and more to journalism.

He and his wife moved constantly, as Lewis became a name in the newspaper world, first to Holywell then to Liverpool, Denbigh and finally to Caernarfon. He contributed to several well-known Welsh magazines and wrote a novel. As his bardic name suggests, Lewis also wrote poetry and published his poems. He was invited to

America to edit *Y Wasg*, a Welsh newspaper read by the many Welsh people who emigrated there during the second half of the 19th century.

This prolific writer also had a pleasant singing voice, and plenty of charisma, so he was in demand to appear at concerts here and in America.

Unfortunately, he was paralysed at the early age of forty seven and spent his final days in poverty, part of the time in Llangefni workhouse. He died at his son's home in Rhyl in 1901 and is buried in Caernarfon, where he did so much of his work. His memorial plaque can be seen on the wall of the Village Hall in Penysarn.

On the wall of the school he attended is the county's memorial to another Penysarn man of letters, Bedwyr Lewis Jones.

He was born in Wrexham while his father, another newspaperman, worked with the Welsh language newspaper, *Y Cymro*, the family went to Llaneilian when he was five and young Bedwyr was sent to the Penysarn school. He had his secondary education at Llangefni where he won a scholarship to the University College in Bangor to read Welsh. After graduating he spent two years at Jesus College, Oxford, then taught for a time at Dolgellau before returning to Bangor as assistant lecturer in the Welsh department where he became head in 1974.

Bedwyr Lewis Jones's influence on the status of Welsh at the University was his great contribution to education in Wales. He was known world-wide wherever Celtic languages were of interest. His personal interests were wide, from sport to craft, social sciences, politics and philosophy. His many Welsh radio talks were hugely popular.

This corner of Anglesey spawned yet another who was to become famous in another sphere. He was Richard Huws, born in Penysarn in 1902. His father was headmaster of Penysarn school and later at Llangoed. Young Richard received his early education at Beaumaris. He showed such prowess when he worked voluntarily during his teens with a local joiner, using his inventive powers to the full, that he obtained an apprenticeship at Cammell-Laird's shipbuilding works on Merseyside where he won a scholarship to study naval architecture at Liverpool University. While studying in the engineering department he attended art classes, an interest which dictated his future direction. Freedom and new experiences beckoned, and he set out to walk across Europe, financing his travels by selling his drawings which found a ready market.

Between 1927 and 1930 Richard Huws studied sculpture in Vienna. He was commissioned to invent and build some unusual constructions. His massive mechanical man, a model of the human body, was a feature of the Glasgow Exhibition of 1938. This was followed in 1951 by a commission for the Festival of Britain. His water bucket sculpture on the Liverpool waterfront was to be a source of delight to many.

Design was Richard Huws's forte. The department of Architecture at Liverpool University employed him to create a far-sighted first year course using his experience in engineering, industrial art and landscape architecture. His days at Liverpool were long remembered by appreciative students.

Between 1955 and 1970 Richard Huws became an industrial design consultant. He returned to Anglesey to live out his retirement, creating a beautiful garden, studying Welsh literature and philosophic and religious thought. His Welshness became increasingly important to him as he aged – he chose to adopt the Welsh form of Hughes as his surname to underline this.

Although a mile and a half away, at the northern end of the parish, Penysarn's parish church is the ancient building near to the coast at Llaneilian. The conical stone tower of the church dates from the 12th century. The remainder of the edifice was rebuilt three centuries later. The chapel of Saint Eilian, at an angle to the chancel, is connected to it by a 17th century passage. The chapel dates from the late 14th or early 15th century and was built on the site of Saint Eilian's cell which was a place of worship in 500 A.D.

The church is full of interest for the visitor. Wood carvings depict angels playing musical instruments; the rood screen has a painting of the grim reaper. Church furnishings are antique.

In days gone by Saints' days were an excuse for celebration. This took many forms, often far removed from worship. 'Gwyliau Mabsaint' (Patronal Festivals) were held at Llaneilian on three Fridays in August. Pedlars flocked to sell their wares. Games and sporting events took place in the churchyard. Inside the church people would attempt to lie in Saint Eilian's chest and if they could turn inside it they could be sure of living for another year. Young people took up the challenge of being able to pass through a division in panelling without touching the sides, to be assured of good fortune. Games of football took place between men of Llaneilian and other parishes. There were no goalposts or rules, merely cross country running, dribbling a ball between two parishes. Often the game would last for the best part of a day.

Llaneilian was the place chosen to base a pilot station where ships sailing into Liverpool Bay could pick up a pilot to guide them in safely. In 1764 eighteen ships were stranded and more than seventy five lives were lost. Liverpool was a busy port, the second busiest in the country. That year seventy four ships left the Mersey for Africa and forty one sailed for America. Two years later the first Liverpool Pilotage Act was passed, and the first pilots were based at a farmhouse near Point Lynas as their lookout post.

A lighthouse was built at Point Lynas by the Mersey Docks and Harbour Board in 1835. Trinity House took responsibility for it in 1973. It was automated in 1989.

There was once a semaphore station on a prominent site nearby. This was the third in a chain of stations from Holyhead to Liverpool. Messages were received from ships approaching Holyhead and sent rapidly along the coast, to be received in Liverpool well before the vessels estimated time of arrival, allowing merchants time to arrange for unloading cargo and a quick turnaround. A copy of the code used, which covered every eventuality, is in the Picton Library in Liverpool. Reading it brings an authentic whiff of the past. The scheme worked well over a number of years before the electric telegraph came into use. Workers manning the stations were very adept at manipulating the wooden arms of the system. But the weather had to be fine for the operator at one station to be sure his signals were readable by the next operator down the line, in this case on Puffin Island.

In 1900 Penysarn received its own telegraph office. This

had been secured by local people being ready to foot the bill and promising to use the facility, as was reported in a local newspaper . . .

At last the telegraph has been established in our midst. By the end of the week many messages will have been sent over the world. Some trouble was experienced in having the service in the area and the cost of the operation will be £24 per annum. The necessary number of people have now promised the obligatory sum to the government. The lines will be available to us for use for one year, on an experimental basis. Will we have to bid them farewell at the end of this period, after all our trouble? I do not believe so. The conveyance charge is cheap enough; only six pence a message. You would have to pay a boy that much to take your message to Amlwch. I believe the neighbourhood will welcome the new station, from Point Lynas to Penygraigwen, and from Mona Mines to Penrhoslligwy. The cost should not lie heavily on anyone and there should be enough custom for the service to pay its way. From now on we hope traders, preachers, our nobility and our commercial enterprises, our sailors and miners, will remember the Penysarn telegraph. The family of Mrs Thomas will have learned to operate it within a week.

Moelfre

Moelfre is a village of sharp contrasts, depending on the weather. The illustrations accompanying this chapter of *Anglesey Villages* shows Moelfre in holiday mood, when the sea is calm and sparkling in sunlight. Yet nature can be so fickle. Next day the picture could be very different, with a gale-force wind whipping up the waves and ships seeking shelter in the bay.

Ships of all kinds have sheltered here since the early invaders – Vikings and Irish, pirate ships lying in wait to attack during Elizabethan and Stuart times, smugglers from the Isle of Man. When Liverpool shipping trade experienced such a great increase in the early 19th century, emigrant ships and merchantmen would shelter before making for port or leaving British shores on their way to ports around the world. And the bay was busy constantly with small, local cargo ships carrying copper, slate and stone. As the weather changed suddenly and unpredictably some ships were caught out and wrecks were frequent.

Before the middle of the last century Moelfre only consisted of a harbour, scattered cottages, a small ship building industry. Men worked on the land, fished, went to sea or helped to build boats. Present-day Moelfre has developed as Anglesey has become a mecca for tourists, many of the visitors eventually choosing to live permanently in the new estates built by enterprising developers who saw the trend.

In days gone by sea rescues were made in poor weather. Today's lifeboat crew based at Moelfre could be called out in any weather, as some yachtsmen do not give enough credence to weather forecasts and do not practise good seamanship.

Experienced sailors deplore the dinghy-weekenders who have never joined sailing clubs to learn the basics of sailing – and surviving – and to appreciate just how dangerous the sea can be. There are holiday accidents among adults and children in inflatable dinghies, rowing boats and power craft. Every lifeboatman will say one cannot over-emphasise the tragic possibilities.

Before the first lifeboat arrived for duty at Moelfre in the mid-1800s, losses at sea off the coast of Anglesey were alarming. In 1825 fourteen ships were wrecked off the coast. In 1826 the number rose to 25, and in 1827 twenty-one were wrecked.

The story of the development of the lifeboat service in Anglesey has already been related, describing the part played by Rev. James Williams and his wife at Llanfairynghornwy. The R.N.L.I. records that the first lifeboat began service in Moelfre in 1830.

Log books report many rescues since then. Moelfre is closely associated with the Institution's splendid record of rescues and the bravery of successive crews over more than a century.

The greatest tragedy at sea on this rocky coast was that of the *Royal Charter* which was lost during a hurricane in October 1859. She had been built at Sandycroft on the Dee in 1855, for the Australia run, and was on the last stage of her voyage home to Liverpool when unprecedented weather suddenly broke all around the coasts of Britain.

It was a night with hurricane-force winds, when 138 ships sank, 90 were damaged, and around 800 lives were lost at sea.

Royal Charter was bringing home 390 passengers, many carrying with them fortunes amassed during the Australian gold rush. The ship also carried over £300,000 worth of bullion.

She hit the rocks at Porth Helaeth, to the north of Moelfre. Although land was so close, seas were so mountainous and winds so fierce that the lifeboat could not be launched and nothing could be done to save the ship.

As bodies were washed ashore they were taken to two local churches, at Llanallgo and Llaneugrad, for identification.

The rector of Llanallgo, Stephen Roose Hughes, and his brother, Hugh Robert Hughes, curate at Llaneugrad, officiated at the funerals of 140 victims at both churches, and wrote hundreds of letters to the bereaved. The tragedy affected the rector's health and his passionate concern was said to have attributed to his own death at an early age.

The bodies of the remaining victims of the wreck were never recovered. As time passed, gold and valuables were washed ashore, and the Crown enlisted the help of twenty men to collect the treasure. A memorial stone on the cliff top close to Porth Helaeth marks the place where *Royal Charter* met her fate.

The Moelfre lifeboat had a vital part to play in another

rescue almost one hundred years to the day of the *Royal Charter* disaster. Hurricane-force gusts of more than 100 mph were blowing in October 1959 when the 506-tonnes *S.S. Hindlea* sailing from Runcorn to Newport in South Wales anchored in Dulas Bay as the wind suddenly veered from south to north. The sea was so rough that the depth from crest to trough of a wave was as much as 25ft. Moelfre lifeboat went to the rescue of *Hindlea* as she dragged to the rocky shore a mile and a half north of Moelfre island. The boat made several attempts to take off the eight men aboard, and coxswain Dick Evans, now a legendary figure in Anglesey's lifeboat history, made ten runs until all were safe. *Hindlea* broke in half on the rocks shortly after the last crew member was rescued.

Those who remember living in Moelfre during the 1939-45 war recall occasions when the lifeboat went out to rescue air crew after their aircraft had crashed into the sea.

Over the years there have been many medals awarded by the R.N.L.I. to crew members of the Moelfre lifeboat, their citations reading like adventure stories.

The latest attraction for tourists at Moelfre is the purpose-built Seawatch centre, which reminds visitors of the importance of the sea to the village, and to the coast around the island. The anchor of the ill-fated *Hindlea* is on show. A modern lifeboat gives children a hands-on experience as they are invited to test the controls and learn of the work of the crew. Displays describe marine wildlife, and a remote-controlled camera brings to life the spectacular off-shore scenery. *Seawatch* is one of the museums in the care of the Museums and Culture Service of Isle of Anglesey County Council.

Traeth Bychan, to the south of Moelfre, was where the

submarine *Thetis* was grounded after failing to surface in Liverpool Bay during trials in 1939.

Visitors to Moelfre during the long, lazy days of summer take home memories of the little harbour, that sparkling sea, and the lush green countryside which is the back-drop to this picture-postcard village. As did the Anglesey naturalist T.G. Walker who spent a weekend here in 1947 and left us a colourful word picture . . .

The light green of the young corn, the strong olive of meadows and pastures, the deeper hues of hawthorn hedges and the reds and browns of the fields all combine to transform the country into a land of lovely patches, brightened by clumps of gold where the gorse had survived the winter. Violets, speedwells, daisies and buttercups adorned both field and hedgerow, and close to the shore, where the tumbling banks slope down to the rocks, there spread a profusion of primroses, celandines, common scurvy grass and blue scilla, outmatching the best of nursery-reared rock plants in their very simplicity and rare beauty of setting. Seathrift bore bright little pink buttons, not having yet attained maturity; neither had the trefoil fully opened; but I did find in the old quarry a host of wild strawberries at their very best, in company with red campion and Herb Roberts.

The sky was colourful and rich, great clouds casting purple shadows on the sea which was itself of intense blue but flecked with white where the current and the floodtide broke against the swiftly running ripples. It was a perfect weekend that I spent at Moelfre during Whitsuntide 1947.

More than fifty years on the picture is still the same.

Pentraeth

George Borrow, in his *Wild Wales*, refers to the village of Pentraeth on Anglesey's east coast as Pentraeth Coch. The name of the pretty bay a mile away is known by every tourist as Red Wharf Bay (Traeth Coch). In time gone by the tides washed closer to the village than they do today and this is when the cluster of cottages around the church and the inn became Pentraeth (the head of the strand).

Borrow's description of his reception at the village inn and the troublesome night he passed in a bed too short for comfort gives a humorous picture of the tourist trade in the Anglesey of his day.

From the cross roads at the centre of Pentraeth one way leads in the direction of Beaumaris. A lane fringed with trees leaves it a short way on the left, and meanders down to a low stone bridge over the river Nodwydd where it empties into the bay through a salt marsh. Here one can watch wading birds and gaze out to the sea which, so often at low tide, is a gleaming strip of water on the horizon. The left bank of Traeth Coch was once a busy little port and had a small but thriving shipbuilding industry. Difficult to appreciate now, when all is so peaceful. To the right, overlooking the bay, rises Mynydd Llwydiarth, a large rocky outcrop now covered by trees but which was once populated in hut circles by Iron Age inhabitants. The overgrown remains of their dwellings, close to an Iron Age fort, are now the haunt of buzzards and ravens.

Close to the village but hidden from it by woods stands Plas Gwyn. Samuel Lewis in his *Topographical Dictionary of Wales* refers to the house as 'a spacious and handsome mansion surrounded by thriving woods and plantations'.

Another writer, in the Shell Guide, comments that the house, The White Mansion, was inappropriately named as it is an imposing red brick, white sash-windowed Georgian house 'which seems to have escaped from Herefordshire'.

Plas Gwyn was built by William Jones between 1740 and 1750 and became the home of the Panton family whose name appears on the public house near the cross roads. In 1756 Jane, William Jones's daughter, married Paul Panton of Bagillt in Flintshire, a barrister and antiquarian. He was educated at Westminster School and Cambridge University. The couple shared their time between Flintshire and Anglesey and were deeply involved in society in both places. When William Jones died, Plas Gwyn was left to Jane. Paul Panton was Sheriff of Flintshire in 1770, and held the same office in Anglesey the following year. He travelled widely in Wales, England and Scotland, and was interested in history and antiquities of all kinds. He collected manuscripts, read early Welsh literature, and gathered a valuable library of over ninety books which was kept at Plas Gwyn.

His son, the second Paul Panton (1758-1822) followed his father's interests but spent more time at Plas Gwyn. He, too, was called to the Bar and he worked within the North Wales circuit. He was a leader in Anglesey public life, becoming High Sheriff in 1807. Panton's cultural interests were the same as his father's, adding to them music and printing. He played the violin, and installed a small printing press at his home. He never married, so on his death the line was broken.

The church of St Mary, known earlier as Llanfair Bettws Geraint, dates from the Middle Ages but, like many Anglesey churches, was partly rebuilt in the 1880s, some time after George Borrow's visit in 1862. Borrow described the church as 'a little edifice of some antiquity with a little wing and without a spire . . . situated amidst a grove of trees'. Angharad Llwyd, writing thirty years earlier, records 'a number of paper garlands used to decorate its roof, commemorating the death of unmarried women'.

Three ancient stones near to Plas Gwyn, called 'Einion's Three Leaps' refer to Einion ap Gwalchmai, a poet born in the early years of the thirteenth century, who won the hand of his sweetheart by a leaping contest, a challenge of strength popular in medieval times. The story tells that he left Anglesey later to undertake a pilgrimage abroad, and left half of his wedding ring with his wife, keeping the other half. After many years he returned to Pentraeth, an old man, and unrecognisable. But when he played his harp and revealed his half of the ring he was welcomed and feted.

Near to the cross roads in the village centre lies one of the commemorative plaques and stones erected by Ynys Môn Council to perpetuate the names of its illustrious sons. This is to Ifor Owain Thomas, musician, artist and photographer. Of all his artistic qualities, he is best remembered for his tenor voice.

Ifor Thomas was born at Red Wharf Bay in 1892 but the

family came to live to the mill in Pentraeth where his father wove cloth which he sold at Llangefni market. His mother was a singer who had been well known in Caernarfonshire before her marriage. She was anxious that young Ifor should be musical, so she gave him lessons which were supplemented by further tuition from a Bangor singing teacher.

When he finished his education at the local school Ifor was apprenticed to a joiner, but music was his chief interest. His mother believed in competitive musical challenge and she encouraged him to enter Eisteddfod competitions. At one of the more prestigious, a National Eisteddfod of Wales held in South Wales, Walford Davies who was adjudicating suggested that Ifor should study singing seriously, and urged him to apply to the London colleges for a place. This he did and when he was twenty-two years of age he obtained a scholarship to the Royal College of Music, being placed first out of four hundred competitors.

Ifor Owain Thomas suffered from asthma throughout his life so, although he made two attempts to join the forces, army service was not for him. Throughout the Great War he remained a music student, then went on to study further in Paris and Milan, where he had the opportunity to sing publicly.

In 1920 he married and settled with his family at Worcester Park in Surrey. Five years later he sang at a Promenade concert in the Royal Albert Hall and made four recordings. Long absences from home followed, and these no doubt were the cause of his marriage breakdown. Engagements at the Comedie Francaise and the Paris Opera brought his tenor voice to a wider audience, then he signed a five-month contract with the Metropolitan Quartet of New York. This gave him a taste for the American way of life. The year 1929 saw him returning to Anglesey on holiday. Divorce was finalised, and he decided to return to the Welsh community on the east coast of America who had been so enthusiastic about his success. There he met Mildred Unfried, a pianist, and they married. Mildred was making radio commercials. Ifor continued to sing with a male quartet and then formed his own group of Welsh musicians called 'The Four Aces', who were in great demand.

At the end of 1933, however, ill health dogged him and asthma brought his singing career to an end. Then came a complete turn in his career. He became a photographer of some note, obtaining commissions from a well-known American journal, Collier's Magazine. For fifteen years he worked with his camera, photographing many famous people in the public eye, actors, film stars, politicians including Winston Churchill and Roosevelt. On his retirement from the magazine came yet another career change, when he began to paint and this, again, was very successful.

The Welsh community in New York provided all the social life he wished for. During the 1940s he founded the Cymric Society of New York which banded together immigrants and American Welsh people.

Ifor Owain Thomas made his last trip to Anglesey in 1955, and while he was in Pentraeth visiting his family he was admitted to hospital in Bangor for treatment to relieve his asthma. This was unsuccessful. He returned to New York an ill man, and died there on his sixty-fourth birthday, to be mourned by many of the friends he had made as a Welsh exile, and by music lovers on both sides of the Atlantic.

Today, the village of Pentraeth has developed with new housing along the road leading out towards Llangefni, and some light industry and a thriving garden centre in the Benllech direction. A sharp eye will detect what was once Pentraeth's main street, a narrow lane between houses which has been succeeded by a new section of road. Walking along this narrow lane, the visitor will still savour the one-time atmosphere of this pleasant little Anglesey village.

Llanddona, Llanfaes and Llangoed

The south eastern corner of Anglesey which juts out into Liverpool Bay has three villages with interesting stories and associations. They are within a very few miles of each other.

Llanddona perches above the sea on what, at the end of the 19th century, was one of the last remaining common lands in Anglesey. It is a widespread scattering of houses with a lane leading down to the church on the southern shore of Traeth Coch. Even today, the village has a set-apart aura, basking in summer sunshine, but forbidding when storms blow in and the surrounding countryside is shrouded in mist.

The church of St Dona has ancient foundations, but was repaired in the 1840s, and in 1873 was one of several Anglesey churches rebuilt by the clergy, in this case, the Rev. Peter Jones who prided himself on being something of an amateur architect of the same ilk as the Rev. James Williams at Llanfairynghornwy, with whom he was contemporary.

Llanddona has at least two claims to fame. It was once reputed to be the home of witches, at a time when superstition ran high among the folk of Anglesey. And it saw one of the first aerial flights in history.

Writing her chapter on Anglesey folklore in *Hanes Môn*

yn y bedwaredd ganrif ar bymtheg, Elizabeth Williams claims that Llanddona was the most notorious district on the island for its witches.

According to tradition, the influx began when a boat came ashore in Traeth Coch, rudderless and oarless, full of men and women half dead with hunger and thirst. They spoke a language none of the locals could understand – the writer says they could have been Portuguese.

They were eyed with hostility by the villagers as it was the practice to put evildoers in such a boat and push them out to sea where the tide would take them away and wash them on to another shore. But when they landed, the strangers miraculously caused a spring of water to erupt on the shore so they were allowed to stay and build themselves rough places to live. The men lived by smuggling. The women begged, and practised witchcraft. All attempts to catch the smugglers were foiled as each carried a black fly tied in a knot of his neckerchief which was freed when the smuggler was attacked and the fly would blind the opponent, so allowing the smuggler to retreat. The women visited farmhouses to beg for food, and if refused they would call a curse on the housewife. So the newcomers were feared.

One of the older witches, called Bella, caused havoc among the housewives as she changed herself into a hare and would play all kinds of pranks on the farm. One of the villagers was so incensed with the trouble she caused that he took his gun, inserted a silver coin instead of the usual shot as he knew witches were impervious to shot, and fired at her. The witches never troubled the people of Llanddona again.

A true story is that of William Ellis Williams and his

aeronautical experiment, which is commemorated by a plaque on the beach which reads 'Mathematician and Engineer. He experimented with and flew an aircraft on this beach in September 1913'.

William Ellis Williams was a quarryman's son, born in Bethesda, who studied mathematics and physics at the university in Bangor. He was especially interested in the stability of aeroplane gliders. During his research at the university he built small gliders which he fitted with pieces of magnesium. He would then light them before release so that the flight path could be recorded on camera which allowed the speed to be calculated.

Ellis Williams went on to research in Glasgow and Munich before, in 1906, he returned to Bangor as assistant lecturer in physics in his old department, and continued his experiments into aerodynamics. His dream was to build his own aeroplane, which he did. It was a monoplane made of lightweight woods, ash and bamboo, which became known as *The Bamboo Bird*.

His obsession caught the interest of the local wealthy shipbuilder, Henry Rees Davies of Treborth, whose financial contribution of £500 was the first towards enabling him to hire an engine for the aircraft. But where was he to build it, and make an experimental flight? Sir Harry Verney who owned land at Llanddona gave him permission to build a hangar on a field close to the beach, and also to test his aeroplane from there.

The test flight was successful. *The Bamboo Bird* flew to a height of seven feet, flying at thirty seven miles per hour.

The first world war halted any further experimentation while the inventor gave war service at the Vickers factory at Brooklands, but after the war he returned to Bangor where he held the first chair of electrical engineering at the university college.

Today, the only birds which use the long flat beach at Llanddona are the natural variety, but the plaque remains to remind visitors of the historic occasion in 1913 when *The Bamboo Bird* took to the air.

The village, which was once the home of those involved in a profitable herring fishery, is no longer remote. The motor car has seen to that. Now Llanddona welcomes visitors in the summer, those working in the commercial and educational centres of Llangefni and Bangor but choose to live away from the workplace, and those who have chosen to spend their retirement in this peaceful south eastern corner of Anglesey.

Closer to Beaumaris, but slightly away from the shore, Llanfaes is now a quiet backwater, resting on its past. During the early middle ages this was an important commercial centre. Records show that between 1280 and 1290 the number of ships calling at its little port rose from thirty to eighty. There was a busy herring fishery industry here, too. Ships carried agricultural products and general cargo to and from the jetty on the shore of the Menai Strait. It was also the main centre for importing wine from France. The village, half a mile inland, had town status. Fairs were held around the church and the Princes of Wales held court here. A Franciscan friary was set up between the village and the port, the first to be founded in Wales. This is where Joan, Prince Llywelyn's wife, was buried in 1237. The friary remained until 1538 when it was dissolved by Henry VIII as part of his dissolution of the monasteries.

The friary church was converted into a barn, and the

stone coffin of Princess Joan was moved and used, for some two centuries and a half, as a water trough until it was placed in a purpose-built gothic mausoleum in the grounds of the Baron Hill estate by Lord Bulkeley, and later still, moved to the porch of Beaumaris church where it now stands.

A mansion called Fryars was built on the site of the friary. During the second world war the Isle of Wight aircraft and boat company, Saunders Roe Ltd., evacuated most of its workers to the site, and from 1940 the design and drawing office staff were added, to work in the newly built hangars and offices. The local people became accustomed to seeing Catalina flying boats at Llanfaes where they were adapted for use as anti-submarine patrol craft for the R.A.F. There are many still alive and living in the area who recall their wartime experiences in the factory at Llanfaes.

After the war ended the factory transferred to making aluminium parts and pontoons for bridges. Then bus bodies were made here and later, refuse collecting vehicles. Nowadays quiet Llanfaes is regarded as a satellite of Beaumaris which is only 'down the road'.

Llangoed has a pleasant main street of houses, cottages, and chapels leading down to the bridge crossing the river Lleiniog in a village-green setting. The parish church of Saint Cawrdaf is yet another rebuild of an older construction but the north transept of 1612 remains. The church stands apart from the modern village, still with its former village school, a chapel and a terrace of cottages.

Llangoed lies two miles north of Beaumaris. Along the road to the coast, across a narrow marshy valley of the Lleiniog, remains of the ancient castle of Aberlleiniog lie hidden on its mound among dense trees. This was built around 1090. The stone bailey was held by Parliamentarians during the civil war.

The one-time mansion of Cornelyn, standing on a rise overlooking the village, along the narrow lane to Penmon, was once the home of two remarkable sisters.

Edith Ellen Henrietta and Gwendoline Elizabeth Eveleen Massey came from Cheshire, where their parents had a connection with Puddington on the Wirral. As did many other moneyed families of the early 1900s, they moved strictly within their own social circle, hunting, travelling and attending all the social functions where it was necessary to be seen. They followed the usual pursuits of young ladies of their time, but they were more noteworthy than many.

Both were accomplished artists, and they enjoyed needlework. A retainer who remembered them at Cornelyn recalled that they made the lace for the maids' uniform caps. But painting was their forte, especially flower painting.

One sister specialised in pencil drawing, the other in watercolour painting. Today their work can be seen at Oriel Ynys Môn, Llangefni, in a wonderful collection of over five hundred pictures of flowers and plants found growing on Anglesey, the pictures bought at auction at Christie's for £2,000. They were painted during the 1920s and 1930s, much of the work being done in a cottage on the shore near Penmon where they would spend a fortnight at a time during the summer. The gallery now owns the copyright of these pictures and has introduced prints of some of them to the gallery shop where they are snapped up by discerning buyers.

Gwendoline created two scrapbooks, now in the archives of the University of Wales at Bangor. They are a delight to see. She wrote them in a large, clear hand, in black ink on white boards, which were bound together to make two large volumes. These are full of drawings and photographs of local people and places. One of the books deals solely with the Anglesey Hunt, prefaced by a large photograph of Gwendoline's sister Edith dressed in riding habit, wearing a bowler with a face veil and a bunch of violets in her coat lapel below her stock pin, standing by her horse.

Details of all the local hunts are recorded, along with anecdotes and memories of hunting personalities on Anglesey. But the chief attraction of these two volumes is their lavish decoration. Gwendoline illuminated the capitals, and designed a riot of wild animals tumbling down the margins and across the bottom of the pages. No expense was spared – she used gold leaf abundantly. Her foxes and rabbits are all gold, with rivetting red glass eyes. What enjoyment she must have had, collating her scrapbooks. They are among the treasures of Anglesey's past.

The plants and flowers Gwendoline and Edith Ellen drew and painted are a wonderful record of the natural history of Anglesey in the early years of the last century.

In the vicinity of the village of Llangoed lies Mariandyrys, a stretch of limestone grassland and heath acquired in 1980 by the North Wales Wildlife Trust, one of six reserves on the island. This reserve covers fifteen acres of a small hill of carboniferous limestone where the most important habitats are limestone grassland, calcareous heath, exposed limestone and scrub with scattered trees.

The reserve area is 'common land for the extraction of firewood' and leased to the Trust, but this ancient right is largely forgotten. A small quarry there was worked until 1950. The most widespread habitat is heathland where heather and gorse grow. Visitors have recorded over two hundred plant species at Mariandyrys.

This is the place to see butterflies of all kinds, over twenty species and over eighty species of moth. Snails abound and so do over thirty species of birds. Lizards and adders make their homes among the gorse. Woodmice, rabbits, hares, hedgehogs, foxes, pipistrelle bats and stoats have been seen. At Mariandyrys rabbits are welcomed as they keep down the fast-growing grasses which might otherwise outgrow the grassland herbs.

There are three entrances to the nature reserve, all quite close to Llangoed and Glan-yr-afon. An explanatory leaflet from the North Wales Wildlife Trust's Bangor office describes the site in detail and gives a helpful indication of what the visitor might expect to find.

Further reading

Dictionary of Welsh Biography
Dictionary of National Biography
John L. Williams: *Llanfair Pwllgwyngyll, Hen Enwau a lluniau'r lle*
Margaret Hughes: *Anglesey Sketches, Anglesey Remembers, Anglesey from the Sea, Anglesey 1900*
Henry Glazebrook & Norman Sheldrick: *Anglesey and the North*
Wales Coast Book
Rev. O. Hughes: *Hanes Plwyf Trefdraeth*
Menter Môn: various brochures for tourists
William Cathrall: *The County of Anglesey*
E.A. Williams: *The Day Before Yesterday*
S. Lewis: *Topographical Dictionary of Wales*
Anthony Carr: *Medieval Anglesey*
Anglesey County Council: *New Bridge over the River Ffraw*
Angharad Llwyd: *Island of Mona*
Owen Williamson: *Hanes Niwbwrch*
J. Hughes: *The Prichard-Jones Institute*
Hugh Owen: *Hanes Plwyf Niwbwrch ym Môn*
R.C.A.M.: *Royal Commission on Ancient Monuments: Anglesey*
Transactions of the Anglesey Antiquarian Society: various
Shell Guide to North Wales
G. Nicholson: *Cambrian Travellers Guide*
Emlyn Richards: *Neuadd Bentref Cemaes*
'Cymru' September 1902
'Rhosneigr Then and Now'
Arch. Camb. Transactions, various
Gwilym T. Jones and Tomos Roberts: *Enwau Lleoedd Môn*

Geoffrey Wilson: *The Old Telegraphs*
Roy Sloan: *Early Aviation in North Wales*
Huw Roberts, Llio Rhydderch: *Telynorion Llannerchymedd*
Eryl Wyn Rowlands: *Ar Ei Ganfed*
Filson Young: *A house in Anglesey*
John Skinner: *Ten Days Tour through the Isle of Anglesey*
George Borrow: *Wild Wales*
Charles G. Harper: *The Holyhead Road*
Aled Eames: *Rescue, 150 years of Moelfre Lifeboats*
Peter E. Baughan: *The North Wales coast railway*